كتاب السير

KITAB AL- SIYAR AL- SAGHIR

MUSLIM INTERNATIONAL LAW

Muhammad Ibn al Hasan al Shaybani

Qadeem Press

Qadeem Press

Qadeem Press Edition
Breathing Life into Forgotten Pages
www.qadeempress.com

Reprinted by Qadeem Press in 2025

Find our titles on your favourite online bookstore using the keyword 'Qadeem Press'

Contents

Dedication.....5

Foreword.....7

Preface.....13

Introduction.....19

The Shorter book On International Muslim Law.....77

Chapter I : Instructions of the Prophet about the Conduct of War and International Relations.....79

Section: Prohibition of warlike operations during the sacred months has been abrogated.....86

Chapter II : The army's treatment of the Disbelievers.....87

Chapter III : Acquisition of Muslim property earlier taken away by non-Muslims as Booty.....92

Chapter IV: Management of *Kharaj*.....101

Chapter V: Peace, Reconciliation and Armistice among Rulers.....104

Section: Agreement of peace on the condition that Muslims should pay a particular amount annually to the disbelievers......105

Section: Acceptance of the evidence of the People of the Guarantee in favour of the heirs of a *Musta'min* who dies in our territory while the Heirs are still in the Territory of War.....107

Section: A *Harbi* found in the Territory of Islam claiming to be an envoy.....109

Chapter VI: Inter-marriages of the people of war and the entry of the traders in their territory with a permission of security.....111

Section: When the people of this territory acquire captives from amongst the other *Harbis*....111

Chapter VII : Injunctions about the Apostates....114

Section: When a group of the *Guaranteed Citizens* break the covenant:....121

Section: When A Case breaks the covenant. 124

Chapter VIII : The Rebels 125

Section: Some virtues of 'Ali (may Allah be pleased with him) 125

Section: Records of the courts of the People of rebellion are not admissible. 128

Section: Validity of the judgement of the Qādī appointed by the *People of rebellion.* 133

Chapter IX: Another chapter on Booty....135

Section: Six questions answered by Abū Ḥanīfah. 135

Section: All freemen taken prisoners by the enemy shall be considered free as soon as the enemy enters the fold of Islam....138

Notes and references....143

Bibliography 179

Dedication

This work is respectfully dedicated to Dr Muhammad Hamidullah, the Shaybānī of the twentieth century. He recodified the *International Law* of Islam in the context of the present century as *Imam* Muhammad ibn al-Hasan al-Shaybānī had done in the context of the eighth century. The work of the Shaybānī of the eighth century is dedicated to the Shaybānī of the twentieth century!

Mahmood Ahmad Ghazi

Foreword

Of the major religious communities of the world perhaps none has had to concern itself with the complexities of international relationship as soon after its inception and to as great an extent as the Muslims. From the very outset the historical career of Muslims has been marked by a high degree of involvement with other political entities, entailing a wide variety of relationships ranging from armed conflict to cooperation and friendly alliance. At the same time, Islam had fostered an attitude of mind which prompted the Muslims to judge matters primarily in the light of their religious norms. The questions which they faced in the field of international relations were no exception to this. In facts we find that the Prophet (peace be on him) and the early Caliphs had to engage in a series of wars and to contend with scores of vexing problems in their relationship with other communities.

As a result, even in the span of a few decades the Muslims had accumulated a considerable wealth of precedents to guide them in grappling with questions of war and peace and the related problems arising therefrom. Also, because of their peculiar intellectual orientation, the Muslims considered themselves bound by certain norms rather than free to pursue their collective self-interest, untrammeled by religious compunctions. To cite just a few examples: the Muslims considered themselves obligated to observe a number of principles even when they were engaged in warfare, to abide faithfully by the agreements they had concluded, and to honor the safe-conduct granted to non-Muslims even by ordinary Muslims. Likewise, even during active hostilities, the Muslims were required to make a clear distinction between combatants and non-combatants and considered it unlawful to kill the latter. They also considered it sinful to destroy trees, harvests, livestock, etc., unless dictated by compelling strategic necessity.

It was probably owing to this strong religious influence-eespecially the influence of the life of the Prophet (peace be on him)—on the outlook of the Muslims that the word "*Siyar*" was chosen to designate what has been termed as the Islamic law of nations or Islamic *International Law*.

For this word, as we know, is the plural of *Sirah*, which in its technical usage means the life or the conduct of the Prophet (peace be on him).

While interest in questions pertaining to *International Law* started among the Muslims quite early in their history, the full-fledged development of *Siyar* took place in the circle of jurists who had gathered around Abū Ḥanīfah. Abū Ḥanīfah had himself greatly enriched this branch of law. Rather than deal with the subject in a perfunctory manner, he had formulated his legal opinions on the whole range of questions with which *Siyar* is concerned. It was, however, left to Shaybānī, one of the two most illustrious disciples of Abū Ḥanīfah, to systematize, develop and refine this branch of law into a highly advanced genre of *Fiqh*. The rich contribution of Shaybānī to the development of Islamic *International Law* has lately begun to be recognized both within and outside the world of Islam. It is being increasingly realized that Shaybānī played an exceedingly impactful role on the development of *International Law* as such, so much so that he merits to be considered one of the founders of this branch of law.

Apart from dealing with questions of *International Law* in quite a few of his works, two of Shaybānī's works are exclusively devoted to this subject viz. his *Kitab al-Siyar al-Kabir* and *Kitāb al-Siyar al-Saghir*. Additionally, the section on *Siyar* in Shaybānī's *Kitab al- Asl* is also very substantive. This work, thanks to its translation by Majid Khadduri, is now available in English. As for the two works the *Kabir* and the *Saghir*-the former constitutes a part of al-Shaybānī's famous al-Mabsut. *Al-Siyar al-Kabir* is a very capacious work and deals with questions of *International Law* in great detail. Apart from being a vast treasure house of legal doctrines in the field of *Siyar,* the work is also highly valuable in so far as it illustrates the extraordinary legal acumen of Shaybānī and his own contribution to Islamic *International Law.*

The other work of Shaybānī on the subject -- *al-Siyar al-Saghir* despite being concise and short, is a work of great significance. It is considered to be a record of Abū Ḥanīfah's doctrines on *Siyar* which was dictated to Shaybānī by his senior fellow-disciple, Abu Yusuf. The work reportedly came to the notice of the Syrian jurist, al-Awaza'i who in turn wrote his comments on it, expressing in a succinct form his disagreements with the doctrines of Abū Ḥanīfah on questions of *Siyar.* Subsequently, Abu Yusuf wrote a rejoinder to Awza'i's work in which he defended all except a few doctrines of his master. This has come to be known as *al-Radd 'ala Siyar al-Awza'.* This work, along with the critical comments of Muhammad ibn Idris al-Shafi'ī is preserved in his copious work, *Kitab al-Umm.* Thus, there can be little doubt that Shaybānī's *al-Siyar al-Saghir* was a work of fundamental importance in the field of *Siyar.* The considerable debate which it generated is an index its significance during the formative period of Islamic

International Law. For it is these debates and controversies which greatly led to the growth and refinement of all branches of Islamic law, including *Siyar.*

Despite its importance *al-Siyar al-Saghir* was unavailable in print up until now. It was extant, however, in manuscripts in several countries of the world.

Dr Mahmood Ahmad Ghazi has rendered a yeoman's service to the history of Islamic law and to Islamic scholarship by painstakingly and skillfully establishing an authentic text of this work. This naturally required much effort in obtaining a number of manuscripts from different parts of the world and then carefully comparing them. Apart from that, Dr Ghazi also ably translated this edited text into English. Additionally, he wrote a very erudite and illuminating 'Introduction' to the work in which, apart from introducing Shaybānī and his contribution to *Siyar*, he presents an illuminating survey of the growth of *International Law* among Muslims, particularly highlighting the very significant contribution made to this field by Shaybānī. Dr Ghazi has accomplished all the tasks on which he had embarked in connection with this work with remarkable ability.

The present work forms part of the series called the Hundred Great Works of Islamic Civilization. The series was initiated by the National Hijrah Council which produced several classics along with their English translations. The publication of this series continued until 1993 when the Hijrah Council was abolished. The Islamic Research Institute, International Islamic University, Islamabad was, however, subsequently asked to take over the Great Books Project.

The Institute feels proud to present, under its auspices, this highly important book along with its translation as the first work in the series. While sending this work to the press, we hope and pray that the Institute would be able to live up to the expectations centered around it and to continue the series as part of the Muslim *ummah's* striving to discover its historical and cultural roots and to put Islamic civilization at its proper place in the cultural map of the world.

Zafar Ishaq Ansari

Islamabad

August, 1998.

Preface

The Muslim world is passing through a crisis that has several dimensions. For it is at once a crisis of identity, a crisis of economic viability and political survival, a crisis of culture and civilization, and, above all, a crisis of thought and belief. It seems that an intellectual void is facing the Muslim *ummah,* which appears hard to be filled. The present conflict and tension in the Muslim world are attributable, in large measure, to the push and pull of the forces contending to fill this void. There is a general feeling in the Muslim world that the West is trying to fill this void. Many Muslims around the globe perceive the new world order as merely a neo-colonial project to force the Muslim world into a pre-planned scheme of things in which there will be little scope for them to develop their genius according to their own traditions and values.

It cannot be gainsaid that Muslims are awakening from a deep and long slumber. But at the present, they appear to be only half way to a true self-consciousness and meaningful awakening. The effects of centuries-long inaction will undoubtedly take time to overcome. Many Muslims seem unable to have a clear perception of the future because of the hangover of the past. The Muslims seem at present to be stumbling around in a condition similar to what a person feels soon after waking up when things appear for a while to be somewhat hazy. They do not have as yet a clear perception of what they ought to do and in which direction they ought to move.

In this situation, the *Shari'ah* has an extremely vital role to play in filling the present void and shaping the future of the ummah. There can be no ummah without *Shari'ah,* nor could *Shari'ah* function in abstraction without a tangible body of the ummah that is committed to applying the *Shari'ah.* Both are necessary to each other. At the same time. it is obvious that the pathway of the *Shari'ah* cannot be trodden without the guiding light of Ijtihad. In order to make modern life relevant to and compatible with the *Shari'ah* and to make the *Shari'ah* understandable and enforceable in the modern context, bold and innovative steps need to be taken. We are under an obligation to develop and maintain an independent critical attitude towards the social, economic, scientific and other developments in the world around us. We also need to understand the Shari'ah through its perennial sources in the context of today's existential facts. At the same time, a restatement of the earlier interpretations has to go side by side with a keen and confident recognition of today's global realities.

The need to develop a fresh, vigorous and meaningful understanding of the *Shari'ah* has been stressed by several Muslim thinkers, but most notably by Muhammad Iqbal, the foremost Muslim thinker of the twentieth century. Indeed, he was the first jurist in the modern world of Islam who invited the attention of Muslim scholars to the urgency and relevance of this task and to the realization of Muslim ideals as far back as the early twenties of this century. He advocated a critical study of the legal and juridical concepts of the West with a view to establishing the universal applicability and relevance of the Qur'anic principles to the ever-changing conditions and requirements of human life. This was indeed a colossal task. It required a concerted and dedicated endeavour of several generations of scholars and jurists. Iqbal himself had dreamed of participating in undertaking this pioneering work. He also made an effort to team up with competent scholars to be associated with him for this purpose. Once, he tried to persuade the celebrated Indian *Muhaddith* of the twentieth century, Mawlana Muhammad Anwar Shah Kashmiri, to come over to Lahore and take up this work with him. In his last days, Iqbal tried to attract another young and competent scholar. Sayyid Abu'l A'la Mawdūdī, moved from Hyderabad to Northern India for this purpose. But no sooner had Mawdūdī moved to Punjab in response to Iqbal's invitation than the latter unfortunately passed away. Iqbal's passionate appeal, however, did not go in vain. Several scholars both in and outside the Indian Subcontinent, undertook this work in their respective areas of interest and specialization. Muhammad Hamidullah, 'Abd al-Razzaq Sanhūrī, 'Abd al-Qadir 'Awdah, Abū Zahrah, Mustafa Zarga and Muhammad Taqi Amīni are some of the highly respected names to whom go the credit for pioneering this cause. These illustrious men, among others, have introduced new dimensions to the vast field of Islamic legal thought and research.

Likewise, there is a need to restate not only the principles of Islamic jurisprudence but also the *corpus juris* of Islam in a manner and a style that would invest the legal scholarship of Islam with greater vitality and ensure an appropriate place for it in the mainstream of legal thinking. At the same time, different branches of Islamic law need to be re-codified as independent legal disciplines. An important and major field that calls for scholastic attention of Muslim academics in this regard is the field of Muslim *International Law* or *Siyar,* which was developed by Muslim jurists as an independent legal discipline as early as the middle of the second century of Hijrah.

The significance of re-codifying *Siyar* and developing it into a living, contemporary and vibrant legal discipline can hardly be over- emphasized. In the context of our rapidly shrinking world and the growing aspiration in the Muslim world to make the *Shari'ah* the major, motivating force in the processes of governance and policy-making, the role of Muslim *International Law* becomes vitally important. However, any intellectual effort to revitalize Muslim *International Law*, and any other branch of Islamic law for that matter, must emanate mainly from the basic sources of the *Shari'ah,* namely the Qur'an and the Sunnah. This would ensure not only the continuity of its glorious tradition but would also keep the recent developments integrated in the original framework of the discipline. All new expansion and future development must be accommodated within the parameters of the original framework. In this context the significance of the earliest expositions of the science of *Siyar* is quite obvious.

The legal research and juridical inquiry of Muslim jurists during the first five centuries of Islam provided a theoretical and doctrinal infrastructure for the later expansion of Islamic legal thought. During these centuries, the *International Law* of Islam reached its zenith insofar as its basic doctrinal framework was concerned. The pioneering works produced during these centuries streamlined the subsequent work in almost every part of the Muslim world. However, the period from the tenth to twelfth century of *Hijrah* witnessed a general stagnation in many aspects of life in the Muslim world. *Fiqh* was no exception.

The dawn of the fifteenth century of *Hijrah* has brought in its wake a renewed desire in the Muslim world to take stock of their current situation and review it to seek remedies for past failings. In the intensity of their desire to shed off the negative vestiges of their period of decline, some over-enthusiastic but less far-sighted reformers suggested solutions that often put their effort into disrepute and discredited even some of their genuine and sincere moves. It is therefore, imperative that the spirit of free and independent legal inquiry prevalent in the first five centuries of Islam be revived with its characteristic originality, strict fidelity to the Qur'an and the *Sunnah*, and its life-generating vitality. This revival will hopefully liberate the Muslim mind from the feeling of inferiority or defeatist mentality and will generate the courage to criticize and evaluate anything coming from anywhere on the touchstone of the Qur'an and the *Sunnah*, and above all, will inspire the ummah with confidence in and the relevance of the *Shari'ah* for all times and climes. For this purpose, a serious study of the vast and unparalleled legal treasure is inevitable in order to identify the eternal principles and permanent elements of the *Shari'ah* and distinguish them from the local or temporal factors which are reflected in the understanding of different jurists as a result of their endeavour to relate the *Shari'ah* to their respective environments. This task requires a re- assessment of early juridical works produced during the first five centuries of Islam.

The present volume is a humble contribution to this process. It brings out the work done in the earliest phase of the codification of Islamic law. Being perhaps the earliest extant work on the subject of *International Law* in the history of mankind, this book was authored by the great systematizer of Hanafi *Fiqh*, namely, Muhammad ibn al-Hasan al-Shaybānī (d. 189 AH). This book represents the author's seminal contribution to the subject, which paved the way for several other works in the field. It epitomises, therefore, the genesis of Muslim *International Law*.

It was in view of the obvious significance of this pioneering work, it was included in the Hundred Great Books Project, started by the National *Hijrah* Council about a decade ago under the dynamic leadership of the late Mr. A.K. Brohi. Dr Muhammad Hamidullah, who has contributed a major work on Muslim *International Law*, suggested that I undertake this work. To him, therefore, is this humble effort dedicated.

Before I conclude this preface, it is my pleasant duty to express a profound sense of gratitude to my learned friend, Professor Dr Abdul Qadir Kilic of the Faculty of Elahiyat, University of Istanbul, for his valuable help in procuring microfilms of the manuscripts of *Kitab al- Siyar al-Saghir* preserved in different libraries of Istanbul as a part of Hakim Shahid's *al-Kafi fi Furu' al-Hanafiyyah*. I would be failing in my duty if I did not record my deep personal thanks and a sense of indebtedness to Dr Zafar Ishaq Ansari, who constantly urged me to complete this work, took pains to edit it, suggested improvements in the 'Introduction' as well as in the translation of the text and, finally supervised its printing.

May Allah reward them all.

Mahmood Ahmad Ghazi

Islamabad

August 1998

Introduction

(I)

Western writers on the history of *International Law* generally believe that the Dutch jurist, Hugo Grotius (d. 1645 CE), is the father of the independent discipline called *International Law*. To them, this science is the product of the Christian civilization of Europe, which was pressed by circumstances to develop a set of rules and principles to regulate the relations among the Christian nations of medieval Europe. Such a contention might be true about European international law as it has developed approximately during the last one hundred years, but it certainly fails to account for the development of international law in the world of Islam.

In medieval Europe, 'international' law did not recognize the existence of any non-European and non-Christian power as a subject of such law. For, as we know, prior to the middle of the nineteenth century, no Asian or African state was considered worthy of enjoying any rights or privileges. It was in 1856 that a non-Christian, albeit half- European, state-Ottoman Turkey-was partly recognized as a subject of *International Law*, though some jurists still contended that the Treaty of Paris (March 1856) simply recognized Ottoman Turkey as a European power but not as a subject of *International Law*. Thus, the rest of the world was excluded from the so-called comity of nations because it comprised a group of 'uncivilized' and 'barbarian' nations.

This set of rules, which later developed into the corpus of *International Law*. was initially developed to look after the mutual interests of the Christian nations of Europe vis-à-vis the non-Christian barbarians. These consisted mostly of the Muslim neighbours of Europe who were considered the objects rather than the subjects of those rules. Those rules, however, continued to govern the relationship of European nations *inter se* and, with the passage of time, became a distinct subject of legal studies, which soon developed into an independent legal discipline and came to be known variously as *droit de gens, droit du genre humain*, law of nations, law of foreign policy, etc.

In spite of the rapid expansion of literature on international dealings and their legal aspects, resulting in the emergence of many scholarly writings on the subject, Western scholars of *International Law* have continued to differ on the very fundamental question of whether *International Law* was really law or not. Some of them refused to accept the set of rules governing international relationships between states as law proper since it lacked the basic elements of what could be considered law: it was not promulgated by a definite legislator; it was not enforced by a competent and effective judicial body; and, above all, it was not backed by the sanction to award punishment in the event of its violation. *International Law*, therefore, had to face strong criticism challenging its very existence. It was called the vanishing point of jurisprudence, law only by courtesy, or just quasi-law. Several modern Western scholars of *International Law* appear to be uncomfortable with its present character. A feeling has emerged that *International Law* fails to meet the real needs and requirements of the human race in our time. Basic changes have, therefore, been suggested to emphasize the need to recast the entire corpus of *international law and* transform it into a truly transnational law, a common law of nations, a world law, and a unified inter-social law.

On the other hand, Muslim *International Law*, *Siyar* as it was called, was accepted as law in every sense of the term from the very beginning. From the early stages of its emergence, it has had all the characteristics of law that the European *International Law* lacked. As we shall see later, Muslim *International Law* never faced the problem of lacking proper sanction and judicial forum to adjudicate disputes under it.

Before we proceed further to discuss the early history and development of *Siyar* as an independent legal discipline, separate and distinct from other branches of law, we may profitably analyze its contents and identify the main questions which were discussed in the authoritative works on the subject during the early centuries of Islam.

(II)

Muslim *International Law*, like other branches of Islamic law, is based primarily on the two fundamental sources - the Qur'an and the *Sunnah*. Like other branches of Islamic Law, its rules have been developed in accordance with the conduct or the 'model-example' set by the Prophet Muhammad (peace be on him) in his interaction with non-Muslims. The term *Siyar* (plural of *Sirah*, which literally means conduct or behaviour) itself indicates that the conduct of the Prophet (peace be on him) in his international dealings constitutes the basis on which the detailed rules of law were developed. He fought battles with his enemies; sent envoys and emissaries and wrote letters to his contemporary rulers; received delegations; led his followers, and himself participated in negotiating various treaties and agreements of international import and dealt with the questions of booty, prisoners of war, and acquisition of the enemy property. This entire conduct, coupled with the general principles laid down in the Qur'an, provided the foundation for the branch of knowledge called *Siyar.*

That the *International Law* of Islam always recognized the paramount authority of the Qur'an and the *Sunnah* is well-known. Additionally, it also recognized other traditional sources such as consensus (*ijma*), analogical reasoning (*qiyas*), the practice of the Companions, especially of the four Rightly-guided Caliphs, and their successors, the early Umayyads. Not only that, the *International Law* of Islam also recognized the principle of reciprocity from the very beginning. Based on a number of Qur'anic verses (e.g., 2:194; 42:40-41; 55:60; 60:8-9, etc.) and the practice of the Prophet (peace be on him) and his immediate successors, this principle was put into operation more effectively by the second Caliph, 'Umar, who issued some directives on the basis of reciprocity, often termed by the jurists as *mujazah* or *mu'amalah bi'l-mithl.*

Although a number of principles and maxims existed to regulate the relations between states in many ancient civilizations, these could not become the basis of an elaborate law on the subject. This was mainly because the concept of reciprocity and equality of status, which could provide the ground for the development of a true *International Law* was generally not recognized. Islamic law, on the contrary, can legitimately be credited with recognizing the principle of reciprocity in respect of other political entities. This, as we know, has come to be regarded as one of the fundamental principles for regulating international relations.

Early Muslim writers on *international law covered a wide range of subjects that have a bearing on the international relations of the Islamic state, such as war, peace, neutrality,* and conflict of laws. In the early period, however, Muslim jurists concentrated on questions pertaining to hostilities. This seems to be primarily because the first three centuries of Islam witnessed frequent hostilities between the Muslims and other entities. At this stage, Muslim *International Law* naturally concerned itself with hostilities or the questions arising therefrom. This was so not only in the case of the relations between Muslims and non-Muslims but also in the case of relations among non-Muslims *inter se*. This explains why almost all the early writers on Muslim *International Law* deal mainly with situations arising from hostile relations. This does not mean, however, that Muslim jurists ignored other issues of international relations while discussing issues relating to war. To cite an example: while analyzing the rights of captives and the disposal of the enemy property, the early jurists elaborately discuss questions pertaining to property rights, acquisition of enemy property, jurisdiction, status, conflict of laws, choice of law, etc. Many a legal concept was developed in the course of such detailed discussions.

Some modern writers have tried to show that peaceful relations between the Islamic and non-Muslim states theoretically represented a temporary phase which reflected the realities of life. Otherwise, these scholars maintain, the Islamic state endeavoured to embrace all mankind through conversion or force; and once that ideal was achieved, there would be no need to have any law at all to regulate Islam's relations with other states which will pass out of existence.

On closer examination, however, this logic would seem odd. If it is accepted and applied to other areas of law, it would amount to claiming that eventually, no legal system will be needed anywhere in the world as all legal systems aim to eliminate crime and injustice and, therefore, should be treated as a temporary phase. Likewise, courts, police, law and order agencies, armies and even governments should be considered as merely temporary measures.

Moreover, the Qur'an and the *Sunnah* constitute the perennial sources of guidance for Muslims and represent the immutable core of the law, which confers stability and continuity to the Islamic way of life in a world characterized by change. The fact that the Qur'an and the Sunnah have provided some fundamental principles to regulate the relationships between the Muslims and the non-Muslims in a non- belligerent situation leaves no doubt that the above contention does not carry much weight. A number of verses in the Qur'an lay down that the original and permanent nature of the relationship between Muslims and the non-Muslims is peace and understanding rather than war and hostility. The Qur'an clearly requires that Muslims should opt for peace as soon as the enemy opts for it (8:61). It declares that Muslims are not allowed to take up arms against a people who are neutral; they are required instead to offer peace (4:94). Moreover, it encourages the Muslims to be kind and generous to those who did not fight against the Muslims and did not treat them with injustice (60:8). Similar examples may also be cited from the *Hadith* literature.

It seems that some scholars have wrongly interpreted the verses enjoining the Muslims to undertake *Jihad* against the idolaters of Arabia regarding whom the Qur'an provides for a treatment different from the rest of the non-Muslims. Most Qur'anic verses on the question, particularly those in *Surah al-Tawbah,* which imply continual war with the disbelievers, apply only to the infidels of Arabia, the Prophet's own people and his immediate addressees. These verses have been generalized by some Western scholars and their application has been extended to all categories of non-Muslims.

(III)

Siyar deals with a wide range of issues. It is difficult to enumerate here all the important areas covered by early writers on the subject; however, the following issues are central to the discussions found in the early writings on *Siyar.*

The most important discussion, which involves principles of far- reaching legal consequence, concerns the concept of *Dar* or territorial jurisdiction. Under this concept, Muslim scholars also deal with questions similar to those of jurisdiction in the modern law, the rights and privileges of foreign rulers and citizens, and the extent of their authority and freedom as recognized by the Islamic state. The question of the independence of the states and various degrees of independence also come up for discussion under the concept of *Dar.* The impact of the difference of *Dar,* its change and renunciation involve a host of questions, some of which also fall under what we now call private *International Law.*

War and the effects of war constitute an important subject of the *Siyar* literature. The nature and kinds of wars and their legal implications also come up for discussion. Questions relating to the treatment of enemy property and persons and prisoners of war occupy a prominent place. Booty and its eventual disposal and the resulting questions of ownership and transfer of property acquired during the war also form an important subject of discussion. Diplomatic and commercial relations are mentioned both under the discussion on wars as well as separately.

Since the Islamic state is primarily a religious, or in a broader sense, ideological state, it regulates its relations with and treatment of persons and groups of persons on the basis of their attitude towards Islam and its political authority. Persons coming into contact with the Islamic state have been categorized on this very basis. Those who accept Islam, those who neither accept nor oppose it, those who both reject and oppose, those who reject and fight, and those who accept the religious message of Islam but fight against its political authority, each of these categories are treated distinctly.

The books on *Siyar* also extensively deal with questions relating to private *International Law* and conflict of laws. How far the legal systems of other nations may be recognized as valid or binding is another important question discussed by the authors of the *Siyar* works in the context of such problems as marriage, divorce and properties of alien persons, including the belligerents. Muslim scholars have written independently on this issue, and such writings may undisputedly be considered the earliest attempts at the exposition of the private *International Law* of Islam.

The method of writing on legal issues adopted by Muslim jurists in the early centuries, which was consistently followed by almost all the later jurists who produced original works on the problems of law, was something similar to what is now known as the case method. But the 'cases' before the Muslim jurists were not always actual court cases. They were, rather, hypothetical questions posed by the jurists who discussed innumerable variations of the same 'case' with arguments in support of each ruling given in respect of every possible variation. This was done mainly in order to provide handy solutions relating to any conceivable problem that any one of them might face, solutions that might be used by anyone rulers, judges, or common people. This method of legal scholarship is thrown in broader relief by the absence of any formal legislative body in the Muslim polity. The absence of such a formal body in the Muslim tradition was necessitated by the private as distinct from the governmental provenance of law in Islam. For there has never been in Muslim history any tradition of formal legislation undertaken by a formal body of law-makers. All legislation was done by private jurists in their capacity as scholars, and their legal opinions became acceptable because of the confidence of the community in their scholarship and piety.

Muslim jurists were undoubtedly pioneers in the field of *International Law* in the sense of an independent legal discipline. Muslim jurists of the second century of Islam were the first to have laid the foundations of this new branch of learning. By the middle of the second century Islamic law had developed to such an extent that various branches of law had started evolving as independent legal disciplines. In fact, by that time, not only international law but also constitutional law, administrative, fiscal, procedural laws, and what is now known as comparative law had already acquired the position of distinct and independent legal disciplines. This took place at a time when the civilized world outside the Muslim world had hardly any clear concept of law proper as distinct from Ethics, Politics and Civics. The historical evidence available to us suggests that Muslim jurists had started paying attention to these different branches of law as far back as in the last decades of the first century of Islam.

By the beginning of the second century, these independent branches of law were further developed and soon started becoming distinct from each other and assuming separate titles. As we have already pointed out, Muslim scholars of the early second century adopted the word *Siyar* as the name for that branch of Islamic law, which deals with the relationship of the Muslim community with other international entities and communities. Perhaps the first Muslim jurist to use the term *Siyar* for Muslim *International Law* in any extant legal compendium was Zayd ibn 'Ali (d. 120 AH), to whom the Zaydi school is attributed. His book *al- Majmi' fi'l-Fiqh* is the earliest extant book on Islamic law and can safely be presumed to have been compiled during the early years of the second century of Hijrah. The fact that the author of *al-Majmu'* has adopted the word *Siyar* as the title of the chapter dealing with questions of international relations indicates that the use of the term *Siyar* for this branch of the law was not very recent. We also find that soon, other jurists also began to employ this term to denote the set of rules governing the international relations of the Islamic state. By the middle of the second century, the term had become an accepted appellation for Muslim *International Law.*

According to early Islamic sources, Abū Ḥanīfah (d. 150 AH) was the first Muslim jurist to compose an independent work on *International Law* under the title Kitab *al-Siyar*. Pursuant to the prevalent practice, the teacher dictated the book to his disciples, who compiled and edited their respective notes with additions and modifications. Those to whom the book was dictated included Abu

Yusuf (d. 182 AH), Zufar (d. 158 AH), Asad ibn 'Amr. Hasan ibn Ziyad (d. 204 AH), Hafs ibn Ghiyath, Muḥammad ibn al-Hasan al-Shaybānī (d. 189 AH), 'Afiyah ibn Zayd, and the teacher's own son Hammad (d. 189 AH), a namesake of his illustrious teacher, Hammad ibn Abi Sulayman (d. 120 AH). These editions were known separately by the names of their respective compilers, out of which the editions of Hasan ibn Ziyad, Muhammad ibn al-Hasan al-Shaybānī and Ibrahim al-Fazārī (d. 188 AH.) are well- known. Unfortunately, the earliest book on this subject by Abū Ḥanīfah has not come down to us in its original form. Like his other writings, Kitab *al-Siyar* was also compiled, edited and popularized by his disciples and successors in scholarship, Abu Yusuf and Muhammad ibn al-Hasan al-Shaybānī. The latter prepared a small treatise known as *Kitab al-Siyar al-Saghir*. This book dealt with the opinions and rulings of Abū Ḥanīfah and his major disciples about some of the leading issues and erstwhile burning questions in the field of *International Law*. To that, however, we shall return later.

Of the contemporary scholars of Abū Ḥanīfah, two other renowned jurists are also reported to have written independent books and treatises on *International Law*, namely, Malik ibn Anas (d. 179 AH) and 'Abd al- Rahman al-Awza'ī (d. 157 AH). Of the two, Awza'i's book has been preserved in the form of some fragments and excerpts by a later authority, Muhammad ibn Idris al-Shafi'ī (d. 204 AH). Unfortunately, Abu Yusuf's book has not come down to us, but Ibrahim al-Fazāri's book has now become available, albeit only a part of it through an incomplete manuscript preserved in Qarawiyyin University in Fez, Morocco.

A celebrated jurist and founder of an independent legal school, 'Abd al-Rahman al-Awza'i was considered an authority on

International Law. Settled in what is now known as Beirut, he was frequently exposed to situations in which he was expected to give opinions on problems relating to *International Law.* Situated on the borders of the Muslim empire, Beirut was a centre of intense commercial and diplomatic activity. It was also the center of the Muslim navy, which was engaged in naval operations against Cyprus and other islands where pirates and outlaws took shelter. In such a situation, Awza'i was the nearest available authority to give rulings on issues that came up time and again. Not only the common people and the local authorities but also the central authorities in Damascus and Baghdad sought his opinion on matters of legal significance, particularly in the sphere of international transactions. This had given a position of pre-eminence to Awza'i, and he had acquired a visible distinction over his contemporary scholars in this field. It should not, therefore, astonish us to find that Awza'i expressed public opprobrium against the political authorities, including the caliph himself, whenever he found that a provision of the *International Law* of Islam had been violated.

On the other hand, Abū Ḥanīfah and Shaybānī were originally based in Kufah, a town situated in the hinterland of the Muslim empire where questions of relevance to *International Law* presumably did not arise as frequently as in Syria. The interest of the scholars of the school of Kufah in *International Law* was, therefore, somewhat of a theoretical and academic character. This background would explain the incident that when a copy of Shaybānī's *Kitab al-Siyar al-Saghir* was presented to Awzā'ī, his comment was not very generous. Perhaps he did not expect an Iraqi scholar to write on *international law since he was not likely to have faced problems in that area in real* life. Awza'i is reported to have commented: "What have the people of Iraq to do with the science of *Siyar*? They have no knowledge of *Siyar* because the wars of the Prophet (peace be on him) and his Companions took place in the Hijāz and Syria rather than in Iraq, which was conquered later. This adverse comment was communicated, perhaps luckily, by someone to Shaybānī. This is said to have motivated Shaybānī to attempt a larger compilation on the subject, and thus his subsequent book, namely, *Kitab al-Siyar al- Kabir*, is believed to have come into being.

Abu'l Wafa' al-Afghafi, a recent authority on the history and early exposition of Hanafi jurisprudence, has come out with a strong criticism of Awza'i's comment. Afghafi's criticism may be summarized as follows:

1. It is not correct to say that the wars fought by the Companions were confined to Syria; these were fought in Iraq as well.
2. Several Companions who participated in these wars in the Syrian region later settled in Kufah and became a source of knowledge about their conduct in those wars.
3. In order to know the details of an event, it is not necessary to participate in it.
4. Knowledge about the Muslim conduct of war should not be confined to those who fought in Syria; it may also be drawn from those who operated in the Hijaz, Iraq, Egypt, Persia, Turkey, Africa, India, etc.
5. Abū Ḥanīfah acquired his knowledge of *Siyar* mostly from Sha'bi (d. 120 AH), a student of Abd Allah ibn Umar who had participated in almost all the major battles after that of Uhud. He used to admire the graphic memory and articulation of his disciple, Sha'bi, by saying that he

explained those events as if he had himself participated in them along with the Companions and that he knew more about the details even though it is Ibn 'Umar rather than Sha'bi who had participated in those battles with the Prophet (peace be on him). "Being a student of Sha'bi, Afgháni wonders, "how can Abū Ḥanīfah be expected to possess scanty knowledge about *Siyar*"?

(IV)

Kitab al-Siyar al-Kabir, the major work on *International Law* produced by Shaybānī in response to Awza'i's remarks, soon became very popular throughout the Muslim world and particularly in those areas where the legal views and rulings of Abū Ḥanīfah and his disciples were followed. It was, perhaps, because of its comprehensive character and elaborate treatment of issues that the book eclipsed other writings on the subject. We shall attempt a somewhat fuller introduction to the contents of the book, and its place in the history of the literature on *International Law* shall be attempted later. Before doing so, we shall complete our account of the writings on the subject during the second century.

The *Kitab al-Siyar,* written by Awza'i, was, in fact, a refutation of Abū Ḥanīfah's views and rulings on the subject. The treatise attributed to Awzā'ī appears to be only a summary of a larger work produced by him, probably as a rejoinder to the work of Abū Ḥanīfah. It seems that the original book written by Awza'i has not come down to us. However, its excerpts have been preserved by Shafi'ī in his voluminous *Kitab al- Umm.* In the fragments included by Shafi'ī, Awza'i refutes some of Abū Ḥanīfah's legal opinions on some important issues relating to Muslim *International Law*. These issues, numbering thirty, include the following:

I. distribution of the *ghana'im* (spoils of war);
II. acquisition of the enemy property by an active belligerent;
III. interpretation of various events during the life of the Prophet (peace be on him), which may be considered his normative conduct in dealing with foreign powers and
IV. the lawfulness or otherwise of the extension of the pledge of guarantee to religious communities not mentioned in the Qur'an.

Awza'i disagreed with Abū Ḥanīfah's opinions on these questions. In the absence of the original treatises written by Abū Ḥanīfah and Awza'i, it is difficult to say whether the disagreements of the latter and the former were confined only to the questions that have been mentioned in the work or extended to other questions as well. If the fragments preserved by Shafi'ī represent a faithful summary of the original, it can safely be concluded that the disagreement between the two scholars was confined to a limited number of questions, whereas they agreed on a large number of issues relating to *International Law*.

One interesting point of disagreement between Awza'i and Abū Hanifah is the application of the *Hudud* laws to a *musta'min* (i.e., a non-Muslim belligerent entering the Territory of Islam on a temporary permit of security and safe passage). Abū Ḥanīfah was of the view that if a non-Muslim *Harbi* who enters the Territory of Islam on the permission of security commits a crime liable to *Hadd* punishment, he shall not be awarded *Hadd* punishment; however, in a case of theft or robbery, he will be liable to pay the compensation of the property stolen by him, even if he has lost or consumed it. According to Abū Ḥanīfah, the reason is that a *musta'min* has neither entered into any agreement of peace with the Islamic state nor any guarantee has been provided to him. Awza'i, on the other hand, was of the opinion that such a *musta'min* was liable to *Hadd* punishment. Abū Yusuf supports the opinion of his teacher and argues that the person would not be liable to *Hadd* punishment because he had not yet accepted the supremacy of the Law (*al-Hukm*) and had not yet been granted any guarantee. Abu Yusuf asks Awza'i: "If an emissary or envoy of a non-Muslim ruler commits zina (adultery) in the Islamic state, will you lapidate him? If a *musta'min* commits an offence liable to *Hadd* in the Territory of Islam and goes back to the Territory of War (*Dar al-Ḥarb*) without being punished, will you prosecute and punish him if he comes back to the Territory of Islam (*Dar al-Islam*)?" With the help of such supportive illustrations, Abu Yusuf establishes that the ruling of Abū Ḥanīfah is sound and Awza'i's opinion is weak.

Another important and controversial question in which Awza'i disagreed with Abū Ḥanīfah concerned the *riba* in the Territory of War. Abū Ḥanīfah was of the view that a Muslim may receive money by way of *riba* from a *Harbi* in *Dar al-Harb* because the citizens of *Dar al-Harb* are not bound by the laws of Islam (*ahkam al-Muslimin*), and a Muslim may acquire the latter's property with their consent in any way he likes. In his rejoinder, Awza'i objected to it, saying that *riba* was prohibited everywhere, including *Dar al-Harb*. He referred to the proclamation made by the Prophet (peace be on him) during his Farewell Address, prohibiting all kinds of *riba,* including the outstanding claims of the Time of Ignorance. How can a Muslim, Awza'i wonders, take *riba* from a people whose life and property are inviolable? Abu Yusuf supports Awza'i on this question and disagrees with his own teacher. However, he tries to explain away the position of his teacher.

Another important question of *International Law* that had been under discussion by Muslim jurists in those days was the attitude of the Muslim judiciary to the personal laws of other communities. *Awzā'i* also gives due importance to it and records his disagreement on several questions relating to marriage and divorce which take place outside the Territory of Islam.

Shafi'ī not only reproduces the fragment of Awza'i's book in his *Kitab al-Umm* but also records his own views and comments on the questions in dispute. After mentioning the arguments of both Abū Hanifah and Awza'i, he compares the two arguments and thereafter records his own views on the subject. In most of the cases he mentions, Shafi'ī supports Awza'i in his disagreements with Abū Hanifah.

Awza'i's book also invited the attention of the disciples of Abū Hanifah. His closest and senior-most disciple and associate, Abu Yusuf, came forward to defend his master against the criticism of the Syrian scholars. He wrote a rejoinder to Awza'i under the title *al-Radd 'ala Siyar al-*Awza'i.

Abu Yusuf not only supports most of the opinions expressed by his teacher but, at places, also comes out with harsh criticism of the views held by the critics of his master, particularly Awza'i. At places, Abu Yusuf seems to have succeeded in refuting the views of the Syrian jurist and establishing the opinions of his master on solid grounds.

It seems that Abu Yusuf's comments could not reach *Awza'i* as he passed away before the book came into circulation. However, Shafi'ī took proper notice of the comments and dealt with the subject in the relevant chapters of his book, *Kitāb al-Umm*. Especially in volumes four and seven of *Kitab al-Umm*, we find that Shafi'ī not only criticizes the opinions of Abū Ḥanīfah and adduces arguments in support of his own variant opinions but also seems to have the criticism of Abu Yusuf in mind, which he appears to be indirectly refuting. It will be interesting to compare the writings of these authors, keeping in view the context of the political life of the second-century Hijrah, especially the relations obtaining between the Muslim state and the surrounding non- Muslim powers.

Abū Yusuf's rejoinder to Awza'i represents a fairly detailed criticism of the Syrian jurist. Running into 135 printed pages, the book deals with several important questions of Muslim *International Law*. The important points of disagreement are the following:

I. Can the distribution of the booty take place within the enemy's territory? This question, in fact, stems from another question: How and when does a belligerent acquire a legitimate title over the property of his enemy? According to Abū Ḥanīfah, as soon as *iḥraz* is completed, the legitimate title is acknowledged. By iḥraz Abū Ḥanīfah means full acquisition of a permissible property by a person entitled to such acquisition. In the context of war, the acquisition will be complete with the physical possession of the property and its safe transfer to the Territory of Islam, from where its retrieval by the enemy is no longer possible. In order to support this principle, Abu Yusuf adduced evidence from the practice of the Prophet (peace be on him), whereby he concludes that the title gets matured only by the fulfilment of the requirements of *iḥraz.* On the other hand, both *Awza'ī* and Shafi'ī are of the view that its transfer to the Territory of Islam is not necessary; that as soon as the property of the enemy is captured on the battlefield or elsewhere, its ownership stands transferred to the capturing army. They rely on some incidents in the life of the Prophet (peace be on him), mentioning that he distributed the booty while he was still in the Territory of War, which shows that the transfer of property to the Territory of Islam was not considered necessary.

II. The second important question that engaged the minds of many people in those days was the distinction between the share of a foot soldier and that of a horse rider in the spoils of war. Although the question appears to be trivial today, it posed an important practical problem for the Muslim soldiers engaged in warfare on the different frontiers of the Muslim empire. In a situation where a full-time army was virtually non-existent, the Muslim state had to rely on volunteers who were paid from the spoils of war. In such circumstances, the question of the respective shares of a foot soldier and a horse rider was one of considerable practical importance. According to Abū Ḥanīfah, a foot-soldier would receive one share, while a horse-rider would receive two shares: one share for himself and the other for the upkeep and maintenance of his horse. On the other hand, Awza'i was of the view that a horse rider should get three shares: one for himself and two for his horse. Both of them relied on some earlier authorities about the practice during the days of the Companions and the Successors. An interesting argument advanced by Abū Ḥanīfah in this regard is that he felt disconcerted at a beast being preferred to a Muslim who fights in the way of Allah.

III. The third important question was about the share of women and non-Muslims who took part in fighting. Abū Ḥanīfah did not consider a woman to be entitled to a regular share unless she practically took part in the battle. Awza'i, on the other hand, considered her to be entitled to an equal share in the spoils of war, irrespective of whether she had actually taken part in the battle or had merely helped the army by providing other services, such as medical help, food, etc. The same difference of opinion exists concerning non-Muslims. Abū Ḥanīfah does not approve of any regular share for them, while Awza'i considers them entitled to a regular share on an equal footing with the Muslim soldiers.

IV. Another important question dealt with by Awza'i and Abu Yusuf concerns Muslim women and children who are taken hostages by the enemy during a war with the Muslims. Abū Ḥanīfah did not see any harm in attacking the enemy and disregarding the possibility of any damage or harm to the lives of Muslim hostages. On the other hand, Awza'i, relying on the implicit meaning of a verse of the Qur'an, expresses the view that the Muslim army must refrain from attacking the enemy in such cases. Abu Yusuf defends the opinions of Abū Ḥanīfah and refers to the practice of the Prophet (peace be on him) in some of his battles to support his master's opinions.

V. Another important question concerned the execution of punishments in the enemy's territory. Abū Ḥanīfah does not approve of the execution of punishments while the Muslim army is still in the enemy territory. Awza'i, on the other hand, sees no harm in it. Abu Yusuf defends the view of Abu Ḥanifah and adduces arguments drawn from the sayings of the Companions and the practice of the early times.

VI. However, as pointed out earlier, the most important question on which the two jurists differed was the question of *riba* in the Territory of War. According to Abū Ḥanīfah, a Muslim entering the Territory of War with the permission of security may enter into transactions according to which he could take interest from the citizens of that territory provided the excess payment is received with the consent and agreement of the other party. Awza'i objected to it in strong terms and declared that every kind of *riba* was disallowed in Islam, irrespective of the territory where the transaction took place. Significantly, on this question, Abū Yusuf disagreed with his master and supported the opinion of Awza'i, Abū Yusuf further said that the argument adduced by Abū Ḥanīfah in support of his opinion was not only weak but also contrary to the unanimously held view of the Muslim jurists. However, he further pointed out that he would invalidate such a usurious transaction only where the transfer of the commodities and the prices takes place within the Territory of Islam, meaning thereby that for all practical purposes, he too upholds the view of Abū Ḥanīfah.

VII. According to Abū Ḥanīfah, if a married woman from the Territory of War embraces Islam and moves over to the Territory of Islam, her marriage with her husband will come to an immediate end, and she will not have to undergo any waiting period if she is not pregnant. Awza'i disagrees with this ruling and prescribes a waiting period for such women.

Abu Yusuf again does not support his teacher but agrees with the Syrian jurist.

Several other questions have been discussed in the book by Abū Yusuf, questions on which he supports one or the other jurist on the basis of the evidence available to him.

Apart from these treatises and their rejoinders, we come across three other important books written on the subject during the second and early third centuries. The book entitled *Siyar,* attributed to Waqidi, and the treatises of Ṭabarī and Tahāwī also deserve some mention. The book of Waqidi has supposedly been preserved by Shafi'ī in his *Kitab al-Umm.* The book deals with some important issues in the Muslim *International Law* of that period. Although Shafi'ī has given this material the title of *Siyar al-Waqidi,* yet it is possible that it may only be a part of the original book, consisting of some selected opinions of the author. The book covers some thirty-four pages of a fairly large size, which deal mostly with the issues found in similar works on the subject. On a more careful examination of the material, it appears that Shafi'ī might have selected such opinions and rulings from the original on which he was in agreement with the author.

It is interesting to note that the fragment in Shafi'ī's *Kitāb al-Umm* under the title *Siyar al-Waqidi* does not make any reference at all to Waqidi. Does this mean that Shafi'ī had adopted the views of Waqidi without any criticism? Or, does it mean that this fragment represents Shafi'ī's disagreement with the opinions that might have been expressed by Wăqidi in his original work, which has not come down to us? Or does it mean that the subsequent copyists dropped the original extracts or passages of Waqidi from the original, stating only the opinions mentioned by Shafi'ī? Or was the title *Siyar al-Waqidi* mistakenly given to this chapter by some copyist? Or has some other word in the original been misread as al-Waqidi by a later copyist? Several such possibilities are conceivable. But in the absence of any historical information, it is difficult to arrive at any definite conclusion. *Siyar* al-Waqidi covers some thirty-four pages of the fourth volume of Shafi'ī's *Kitab al-Umm*. It includes 105 reports under some eight headings, which have been reported from Shafi'ī as usual by his student al-Rabi ibn Sulayman al- Murādī. It may be mentioned here that Ṭabarī, in his *Ikhtilaf al-Fuqaha* seems to consider this book to be Shafi'ī's. At four different places in his book, he refers to Shafi'ī as making certain statements in *Siyar al-Waqidi*. If it was a mistake, it had already gained currency during Ṭabarī's time.

Although Ṭabarī and Ṭaḥāwī belong to a later period, the discussions in their respective books on the disagreements among jurists reflect the juridical thinking of the later part of the second century. A glance over their works indicates that the differences of opinion on the issues relevant to Muslim *International Law* during the second and third centuries of *Hijrah* contributed significantly to the emergence of a new legal discipline: the comparative study of law called *Ikhtilaf al-Fuqaha* or the science of the disagreements of jurists.

Ṭabarī's *Ikhtilaf al-Fuqaha*, edited by Joseph Schacht, is a fragment of a larger manuscript. It deals with questions of *jihad, jizyah and hirabah*, three important areas covered by the early writers on the *Siyar*. Although the book does not represent a comprehensive exposition of the *Siyar*, still it covers a wide range of issues, the more important of which are the following:

I. *Jihad,* its philosophy and objective;
II. The laws of war; permissible and forbidden acts during war;
III. those who may and who may not be killed in a battle;
IV. peace and armistice with the non-Muslims; its conditions, duration, etc.;
V. Permissibility of peace agreement in case the enemy is more powerful;
VI. providing guarantees to non-Muslims, their terms and conditions, and the grounds of their nullification; the rights and privileges of the subject; *jizyah and Kharaj* (a subject on which there are some of the longest discussions in the book);
VII. The rights and privileges of the *musta'min*, an alien citizen of a hostile country temporarily entering the Territory of Islam on the permission of security;
VIII. Prisoners of war and their treatment;
IX. enemy persons and enemy property;
X. enforcement or non-enforcement of the law of Islam on an enemy person or *musta'min*;
XI. The territorial character of the jurisdiction of the law of Islam, the execution of Hudud in the Territory of War, and questions relating to the spoils of war and their distribution.
XII. (The subject on which the discussion is the longest); and highwayman ship and robbery. Significantly, the author does not discuss the question of *riddah* or apostasy anywhere in the book.

The book is the first extant work that exclusively deals with a comparative study of the legal rulings of the early Muslim jurists on the question of international law. Where the jurists agree on a particular question, the author mentions it at the beginning of his chapter or discussion. This is followed by the mention of their disagreements on the questions concerned, along with their respective arguments. The jurists whose views have been frequently referred to and discussed are Awza'ī, Abū Ḥanīfah, Malik, Thawri (d. 161 AH), Shafi'ī, Abu Thawr (d. 240 AH), Abu Yusuf, Shaybānī, Hasan ibn Ziyad and Zufar (d. 158 AH). Significantly, the book does not mention Ahmad ibn Hanbal or the disciples of any of the jurists of the second and third centuries except those of Abū Ḥanīfah. Was it because Ṭabarī was influenced by Abū Hanifah in his early career before he founded his own school of *Fiqh*?

V

In the later centuries, the *International Law* of Islam continued to develop as a distinct legal discipline on which books were written by different scholars. During this period, with the emergence of changed political situations, new problems arose, and Muslim scholars tried to grapple with them. This led to a continuous development and expansion of the discipline.

Before concluding this brief account of the contribution of the Muslim jurists in the development of *Siyar*, it seems apt to highlight the points of difference between *Siyar* and modern *International Law* as developed in the West.

1. The most important area of difference between the two systems of law is, perhaps, the question of the validity of the law itself. We have already mentioned that the writers on *International Law* in the West have been discussing the question of whether *International Law* really merits to be called 'law' or not. Some scholars considered it to be no more than positive international morality to be kept in mind in the

course of interaction between states. Some other scholars have called it the vanishing point of jurisprudence. This reluctance to confer upon *International Law* the status of 'law' stems chiefly from the definition of law, for law is conceived by these jurists in terms which tend to deny the status of law to anything not imposed by any superior human authority. Even today, despite great expansion in the field of law and the establishment of institutions such as the International Court of Justice, which has a facade of authority to enforce the rules of *International Law*, there are scholars who are still reluctant to accept *International Law* as *law.*

Muslim scholars, on the contrary, never felt any such difficulty. Their concept of law was different from the one generally recognized in the Western tradition. They developed rules of *International Law* on the basis of the same principle on which rules relating to municipal law were developed. Islamic law, being primarily a religious law which, had its own foundation of authority and legitimacy in the two primary sources, the Qur'an and the *Sunnah.* Muslim jurists never felt uncomfortable in considering both municipal law and *International Law* as parts of the same law, the *corpus juris* of Islam. The sources from which the municipal law draws validity and sanction equally provide legitimacy to the rules of *International Law.* The binding character of the rules of Muslim *International Law* is not based on any reciprocity, mutual consent or any external sanctioning agency. It is basically a self-imposed set of rules invested with moral and religious sanctions. Muslims are bound to follow its principles and apply its rules even if they run counter to their own interests.

2. Since Islamic law was developed by independent jurists rather than the state, its relationship with the existing political authority was different from that of other legal systems. Law, in other traditions, is generally recognized as such only when it is promulgated by the political authority; that is to say, law is always the creation of the political authority of the state apparatus. On the other hand, in the Islamic tradition, it is the other way round: the state and the political authority are the creations of the law. Law preceded the state in Islam not only theoretically but also historically. That is why there has never been any tradition of formal legislation in Muslim history. There have never been any formal bodies in the Muslim states specifically charged with the task of legislation. True, there have been groups of persons known as *Ahl al-Shura* or *Ahl al-Hall wa 'l-'Aqd,* but these neither exercised any legislative authority nor performed any function having a bearing on law-making.

   The development of law in Islam has always been independent of the government. The supreme law, which constituted the ground- norm, was derived from the Qur'an and the *Sunnah.* Anything opposed to this supreme law was null and void and the authority to decide whether a law was or was not *ultra vires* of the supreme law always lay in the hands of the jurists and the jurisconsults. The authority of the courts to make a judicial review of administrative actions and legislative proposals was also based on the authority of the judges as jurists and not *vice versa.*

   Thus, the entire concept of Muslim *International Law* is basically different from that of Western *International Law,* which not only stems from the will of the rulers but also remains contingent upon it. In a sense, Muslim *International Law* has been unilaterally followed by the Muslim states in their relations with their own non-Muslim citizens as well as with the contemporary international communities and entities with which they came into contact.

3. This also throws in bold relief the question of the sanction of *International Law* that was greatly played up by Western authors. The sanction behind Muslim *International Law* is the same, which legitimizes the municipal law of Islam. In that respect, Islamic law does not recognize any distinction between its municipal and international components. The sources of both being the same, the whole notion of there being a different kind of sanction for each of them is out of the question.
4. From the very beginning, a number of scholars have disputed the claim that modern Western *International Law* has a universal character. Early writers on *International Law* in the West have been more candid in their reservations about its universal character. Those who challenged the universal character of Western *International Law* relied on solid historical facts. How can a law which had been conceived to regulate the relations among the Christian states of Europe, they enquired, be regarded as a universally applicable set of rules? For several centuries, its application was recognized as being confined to the civilized nations of Europe. Whether or not the non-European world was civilized is a separate question, but the fact remains that the law was confined to the 'civilized' nations. This was considered a major reason for not recognizing the universal character of this law.

On the contrary, Muslim *International Law,* from the very moment of its birth, has had a universal bearing. Muslims never raised the question of whether someone was civilized or uncivilized, a question on which no clear and commonly accepted criterion could ever be laid down. It rather adopted a criterion which was clearer and more precise in its application, namely the religious and political affiliation of the person concerned. It classified its subjects into categories based on the attitude of people towards Islam, both as a religion and as a political entity.

Even historically, the application of Muslim *International Law* was universal from the very beginning. During the first two centuries of Islam, it was able to regulate the relations of the Muslim state with such diverse sets of peoples, nations and communities as the European Christians of Spain, France and Italy, the Berbers of Morocco, the inhabitants of Ethiopia, the Hindus and Jainis of India, the Buddhists of India and Central Asia and the Taos and Shintos of China and the Far East.

5. Western *International Law* has been confined to the relationship between nations and states. The very nomenclature of international or *inter-statal* suggests that the law is meant only to regulate the relationship between nations and states. For several centuries, it did not recognize individuals, groups, and communities as its subjects-matter. Muslim *International Law*, in contrast, recognized categories from groups and communities as its important subjects from the very beginning. Although Western *International Law* does presently govern, albeit indirectly, the relations of individuals and also recognizes some of their rights and obligations, it does not confer any right on individuals to

invoke its provisions for the protection of their rights. Kelsen is perhaps the first modern jurist of the West who has acknowledged some scope for individuals in his exposition of *International Law.* However, the prevalent practice in the West has not yet given due recognition to the Kelsenian theory of *International Law.* An individual, for example, cannot move the International Court of Justice, the Commission on Human Rights, the Security Council, or such other forums to solicit a remedy provided for in any of the international instruments. Even municipal courts are, in most cases, barred from entertaining such complaints.

On the other hand, Islamic law has never deprived individuals of seeking redress available to them under the rules of Muslim *International Law.* There are instances when individuals moved a municipal court established by a Muslim state and invoked a rule of Muslim *International Law,* thereby securing the remedy provided therein. Not only the citizens of the Muslim state but also the members of a belligerent army and their compatriots had the right to move a Muslim court, invoking a relevant rule of Muslim *International Law.*

It may be pointed out that some Western scholars have now begun to recognize this lacuna in international jurisprudence. There are also indications of a growing plea to widen the scope of *International Law.*

6. Some scholars have shown a tendency to belittle the universal character of Muslim *International Law* by referring to the fact that it was primarily based on a religious message which provided legitimacy to its rules. But if we were to compare the *Siyar* with the Western *International Law* on this count, the approach seems to be much more liberal in Islamic

law. As far as the respective origins of both laws are concerned, they are embedded in their respective religious backgrounds. The Western *International Law*, as conceded by several Christian and Jewish writers, is an offshoot of the Christian civilization prevalent in Christendom. Its entire development took place in the context of Christian Europe, and even today, the Christian imprint is quite visible. Although with the passage of time, the Christian character of European *International Law* has gradually diminished, the fact remains that for centuries, Christianity regulated the relations of the Christian states *inter se.*

The Christian component of Western *International Law* becomes more striking in areas where a rule of *International Law* is disputed by one of the parties. In such a situation, according to a recent but highly respectable authority, Oppenheim, it lays down that the principles of Christian morality should be applied. On the other hand, in a similar situation, Muslim *International Law* does not invoke any principle of Muslim morality. It invokes the principles of natural justice, particularly the principle of *tamathul, mujāzah* or reciprocity, ensuring an equal footing to both parties.

(VI)

Muhammad ibn al-Hasan al-Shaybānī, the author of the present treatise, is one of the triad of authorities in the Hanafi school of law, the other two being his teacher, Abū Ḥanīfah and his senior colleague-cum- teacher, Abu Yusuf. They constitute the nucleus to which goes the credit of laying the foundations of the largest school of Islamic law and jurisprudence. Almost ninety per cent of the rulings given by Abū Hanifah have been reported to us by Shaybānī.

Originally from a town near Damascus. Shaybānī was born around 130-131 AH in Wasit and was brought up in Kufah (Iraq). His father was a wealthy man who served in the army. Shaybānī received his education mostly in Kufah. His teachers include Abū Ḥanīfah, Awzā'ī. Malik ibn Anas, Sufyan al-Thawri and Abu Yusuf. However, the foundation of his scholarship was laid and his legal and juridical understanding was sharpened by Abū Ḥanīfah, whose academy he joined at the age of fourteen. Before that, he had already memorized the Qur'an, studied Arabic language, and acquired a grounding in the science of *Hadith*. His teachers of *Hadith* included authorities like Abu'l-Zinād, Sufyan ibn Uyaynah, Saīd ibn Abi 'Arubah, Shu bah, and Abd Allah ibn al-Mubarak." He then spent only a few years of his life in the company of Abū Ḥanīfah. Shaybānī completed his education mostly at the hands of Abu Yusuf, his senior colleague in the academy of Abū Hanifah. He spent some years in the company of his new teacher, Abū Yusuf, during which period Shaybānī edited, under his guidance, the lectures of Abū Ḥanīfah. But unfortunately, some differences cropped up between the young jurist and his teacher. Abu Yusuf and the association did not last long. It was perhaps after his dissociation from Abu Yusuf that he joined the circles of Awza'i and Sufyan al-Thawrī. However, his association with them was short-lived as he soon went to Hijaz to join the celebrated circle of Malik ibn Anas in Madinah.

He remained with *Imam* Malik for quite some time and completed his study of *Hadith* under him. He also prepared a new version of Imām Malik's *Muwatta'*, which was known after his own name as *Muwatta' Imam Muhammad* to distinguish it from the popular edition of the *Muwatta'*, prepared by the Spanish disciple of the Madinite teacher, Yahya ibn Yahya al-Maṣmūdī. But Shaybānī's version of the book did not become as popular as Yahya's version. The former remained mostly confined to South Asia and Central Asia, where the population is predominantly Hanafi.

Historians have reported an interesting anecdote of Shaybānī's first encounter with *Imam* Malik. When the young Iraqi jurist visited Madinah for the first time, he went *incognito* to the circle of *Imam* Malik and inquired: "What is your opinion about a person who is in need of major ablution (*ghusl*) and who comes to a mosque and finds that the water for ablution is available only in the mosque where a congregational prayer is already in progress?" *Imam* Malik replied, "A person who is in need of major ablution cannot enter the mosque". The young stranger repeated the question several times only to receive the same answer from Imām Malik. Noticing that the young man was not satisfied with the answer. the teacher asked: "What, then, is your opinion?" "He should make tayammum, enter the mosque, obtain water and make ablution to join the prayer", came the prompt answer. Astonished with the clarity and presence of mind of the young visitor, *Imam* Malik asked: "Where are you from?" "From here." (Pointing to the earth), was the answer. When he left the company, *Imam* Malik asked his colleagues as to who the visitor was. When he was told that he was a young disciple of Abū Hanifah from Iraq, he wondered: "But he told me he was from here!" When it was explained to him that while saying so he had pointed to the earth, *Imam* Malik observed that his second answer was even more astonishing and intelligent."

The impact of the Madinan school on Shaybānī's writings is evident from his mastery of the science of *Hadith.* His writings represent a unique combination of rational interpretation of early precedents and a profuse citation of authorities, particularly the sayings and practices of the Prophet (peace be on him) and his Companions.

Shaybānī started his teaching career in Kufah at the age of twenty. The major part of his life was spent in teaching and writing. His students included celebrities like Shafi'ī', Asad ibn Furat, the compiler of the Maliki jurisprudence, Muhammad ibn Muqatil, Yahya ibn Ma'in, the historian Waqidī, and the jurist specializing in public finance, Abū 'Ubayd al-Qasim ibn Sallām. His students were always full of appreciation and praise for his personality and scholarship. Shafi'ī, for example, used to say that after *Imam* Malik, he would recognize only Shaybānī as his true teacher. Once he told his audience that the notes he had prepared in the company of Shaybānī were equal to the load of a He-camel. He would then explain that he was referring to a He-camel because it can carry more weight than a she-camel. Once Shafi'ī observed that he never saw a person more knowledgeable about what is lawful and what is unlawful and the niceties of law than Muhammad ibn al-Hasan al-Shaybānī. Similar observations were made by other disciples of Shaybānī as well. Abu 'Ubayd, for example. is reported to have said that he never came across a person who had more profound knowledge of the Qur'an than Muhammad ibn al-Hasan.

In the later years of his life, Shaybānī came in close contact with the Abbasid caliphate and was soon appointed a judge by Harun al-Rashid in one of the provinces of Iraq. He held this office for quite some time but continued writing even while he was a judge. During this period, he was consulted by the government as well as by the Caliph on important legal issues. Once, he was asked about the lawfulness of an action intended to be taken by the Caliph Harun al-Rashid about the well-known Christian tribe of northern Arabia, Banu Taghlib. This was a very powerful Arab tribe that had settled on the border of Arabia, Iraq, and Syria and had accepted Christianity long before the Prophet (peace be on him). They were recognized by the Eastern Roman Empire as legitimate rulers of a small buffer state in that region. During the Muslim-Christian hostilities in the early years of Islam, the tribe of Banu Taghlib was at the forefront of military opposition to Islam. However, during the reign of Caliph 'Umar, they felt that they were no more in a position to withstand the rising tide of Islam. They decided to give up their hostile posture and entered into a respectable agreement with the Muslims. They recognized the political suzerainty of the Madinan state on the condition that they would not pay *jizyah* but would pay a special tax equal to double the amount of *zakah* payable by the Muslims. They also agreed that they would not prevent their children from accepting Islam.

It was pointed out to Caliph Harun al-Rashid that the Banu Taghlib were not abiding by the conditions and were preventing their children from accepting Islam. Upon this, the Caliph desired to intervene and annul the agreement made with them by the Caliph 'Umar. Shaybānī was consulted on the constitutional validity of such an action by the Caliph. Shaybānī strongly supported the Taghlibites on the plea that even if it was at all a violation of the agreement, it had continued since the time of the Second Caliph. The Rightly Guided Caliphs had not objected to these violations. Therefore,

Shaybānī argued, the practice should be allowed to continue on the ground of *istiṣhab.*

Shaybānī passed away in Rayy in 189 AH, at the age of fifty-eight. His funeral prayer was led by the Caliph Harun himself, who told the gathering that they were not burying the earthly remains of a mortal; they were rather burying the science of law and jurisprudence itself.

(VII)

Shaybānī was perhaps the most prolific writer on jurisprudence during the second century of Hijrah. He produced a vast treasure of writings which virtually covered every area of law. Among his junior contemporaries, it is only Shafi'ī who rivals him in the volume of work left for posterity. No other scholar of that age had such a profound and lasting impact on the legal thinking of the succeeding generations of Muslim jurists as had Shaybānī and Shafi'ī.

Shaybānī left behind a large number of books dealing exclusively with legal problems. His books constitute the basis on which the Hanafi school of law was developed. His contribution to the Hanafi legal tradition is undoubtedly the greatest after that of Abū Ḥanīfah. Even his senior colleague and teacher, Abu Yusuf, has left us only a few works of pure legal nature, and his personal impact on the Hanafi legal thought was decidedly less than that of his younger colleague.

A large number of books have been attributed to Shaybānī by historians and biographers, but not all of them have come down to us. Before we introduce his major works, a mention of the full list of his writings will not be out of place.

A

I. *Kitab al- Jami' al- Saghir.*
II. *Kitab al- Jami' al- Kabir.*
III. *Kitab al- Asl.*
IV. *Kitab al- Siyar al- Saghir.*
V. *Kitab al- Siyar al- Kabir.*
VI. *Kitab al- Ziyādāt.*

B

VII. *Ziyadat al- Ziyadat.*
VIII. *Kitab al- Hujjah 'ala Ahl al- Madinah.*
IX. *Muwatta' al- Shaybānī.*
X. *Kitab al- Athár*
XI. *Kitab al- Makharij wa'l- Hiyal.*
XII. *Kitab al- Amali*

C

XIII. *Raqqiyyat*
XIV. *Jurjāniyvät.*
XV. *Kitab al- Nawadir.*
XVI. *Kitab al- Kasb.*
XVII. *Kitab al- Buyu.*
XVIII. *Kitab Ijtihad al- Ray.*
XIX. *Book of al- Istihsan.*
XX. *Kitab al- Hujaj.*
XXI. *Kitab al- Kharaj.*
XXII. *Kitab Usul al- Fiqh.*

The six works mentioned under 'A' are known as the books *of Zahir al-Riwayah* and constitute the foundation on which the edifice of Hanafi jurisprudence rests. The two 'short treatises', namely *al-Jami' al- Saghir* and *al-Siyar al-Saghir*, were written by him in his early career when he was still busy completing his higher legal studies under Abū Yusuf. It seems that both the books were written in the early years that followed the death of Abū Ḥanīfah, i.e.,,, between 150 AH and 157 AH, the year when Awza'i passed away. Both these books were presumably compiled under the patronage and guidance of Abu Yusuf who seems to have dictated the major parts of the two. As to the two 'long treatises', namely, *al-Jami' al-Kabir* and *al-Siyar al-Kabir*, they appear to have been written at a later stage when the author was able to make his own exposition of the law in a mature way.

Al-Jami' al-Saghir is a concise text embodying some 1532 important legal questions relating to a variety of subjects covering almost the entire spectrum of Fiqh. These issues are mostly those where apparently there is no difference of opinion among the three Hanafi jurists, namely, Abu Ḥanifah, Abu Yusuf and Shaybānī, whose views have been preserved in the book. Only 170 issues are such that these early scholars have disagreements on. Almost all the rulings included in the book are based on the authoritative sources the Qur'an, the traditions of the Holy Prophet (peace be on him), and the practice of the Companions and the Successors. Only a couple of rulings are based on secondary sources like *qiyas* and *istiḥsan.*

Although the evidence at our disposal suggests that the book was written during the early career of Shaybānī, as mentioned earlier, an erudite scholar of our own time, Muhammad Zahid al-Kawtharī, is of the view that it was written after *Kitab al-Asl* which, on account of its depth and maturity, appears to have been written somewhat later. According to Kawthari, after Shaybānī completed his *al-Asl*, he was requested by Abu Yusuf to prepare a handy volume consisting of a summary of the legal opinions of Abū Ḥanīfah as transmitted to Shaybānī by Abū Yusuf. The book was liked by Abu Yusuf to such an extent that he is reported to have always kept it with him even during his travels.

Strangely, the book could not become very popular as a text-book perhaps because other texts that appeared during the third and the fourth centuries caught the imagination of the academic community on account of the latter's precision and improved presentation, and, especially their capacity to be used by students. Notwithstanding that, the book has always been very popular as a source book and many commentaries were written upon it, the more recent and popular being the one by Abd al- Hayy Lakhnawi, *al-Nafi' al-Kabir.*

The sister volume of the work, *al-Jami' al-Kabir*, is considered to be one of the best books of Shaybānī, which ensured him a highly respectable and lasting position in the history of Islamic law and jurisprudence. Some scholars have even hailed it as the best work written on Islamic law (presumably during the early centuries of Islam). Jurists of other schools have also acknowledged the greatness of the effort. Ibn Taymiyyah, for example, is reported to have been impressed by the erudition of Shaybānī as reflected in this work, especially where the author discusses the questions of Arabic grammar and lexicon in the course of his discussion of legal issues.

The book has been quite popular, and several commentaries on it have been written by different scholars. Unfortunately, these commentaries have not yet seen the light of the day; most of the manuscripts are preserved in various libraries of Istanbul.

Kitab al-Asl is one of the earlier works of Shaybānī, which was probably compiled under the guidance of Abu Yusuf. It is also one of the most voluminous works, if not his most voluminous work. Perhaps because of its size, it was also known as *Kitab al-Mabsut*. It is said that Shafi'ī had memorized it, and it was after having thoroughly absorbed this book that he set off to write *his magnum opus, Kitab al-Umm*. It is also reported that a jurist, who was originally a Jew, had accepted Islam after going through this book, saying that if the work of the junior Muhammad [al-Shaybānī] was of such greatness, how great would have been the work of the senior Muhammad (peace be on him)!

Running into several volumes, *Kitab al-Asl* deals with tens of thousands of legal questions that were hypothetically posed by the circle of Abū Ḥanīfah, discussed by them at length and then final positions in respect of them was formulated. An answer was formulated in response to every legal question that was posed along with the arguments in support of the ruling of his school, either by citing an earlier authority (a *hadith*, *athar*, or any other traditional evidence) or by recourse to analogical reasoning in the absence of traditional material directly relevant to the legal question concerned. In many cases where the authority in support of a ruling was well-known and considered authentic in the juristic circles of his generation, particularly in Iraq, Shaybānī skipped over the authority which he took care to mention in those cases where he felt that the relevant authoritative material was not widely known.

Being one of his earlier writings, in his *Kitab al- Asl* Shaybānī mostly confines himself to mentioning the views of Abū Ḥanifah and Abū Yusuf; however, at certain places where he disagrees with the views of his master, he specifically mentions his own views as well. Until recently, *Kitab al-Asl* was available only in manuscripts preserved in various libraries of Istanbul and Cairo, but now it has been published.

Al-Ziyādāt, another work of Shaybānī, was written long after the completion of *al-Jami' al-Kabir* and was meant to be its complementary volume. It includes his rulings on some new questions and situations he contemplated after the writing of *al-Jami' al-Kabir.*As for the two books on *Siyar*, we shall come to them later.

The six books mentioned under 'A' provided the foundation on which the later scholars constructed the legal corpus of the Hanafi school. It appears that these works soon became the source of basic knowledge about the Hanafi rulings and gained popularity in scholarly circles, particularly in the lands where Hanafi legal doctrines were followed. In order to facilitate students in attaining mastery over the contents of these books and thereby gaining access to the underlying principles of Hanafi law, a jurist of the fourth century, al-Hakim al-Shahid Muḥammad ibn Muhammad al-Hanafi al-Marwazî, prepared their summary known as al-Kafi fi Furu' al-Hanafiyyah. This work soon became popular as a textbook, particularly in the central and southern Asian regions where Hanafi *fiqh* was predominant. *Al-Hakim al-Shahid al-Marwazi,* while summarizing the contents of the rest of the five books, had included *al-Siyar al-Saghir* as it is, perhaps because he found that *al-Siyar al-*

Saghir already represented a good summary of the author's writings on the subject.

Later, the well-known Hanafi jurist of the fifth century of *Hijrah*, Shams al-*Din* Muhammad ibn Ahmad ibn Sahl al-Sarakhsi (d. 483 AH) wrote a commentary on *al-Kafl* which runs into thirty volumes and was dictated while he had been imprisoned by a local ruler of Awzjand (which is a part of present-day Uzbekistan), in a dried-up well. This voluminous work, known as *al-Mabsut*, is considered one of the most popular and authoritative expositions of Islamic Law as understood and expounded by the Hanafi jurists.

Other works of Shaybäni mentioned under 'B' and 'C' are known as the books of *Nadir al-Riwayah* and are considered to be of secondary importance in comparison to the group of books called *Zahir al-Riwayah* which were considered the most authoritative sources of the Hanafi legal doctrines. However, these books (mentioned under 'B' and 'C'), along with the writings of the other students of Abū Ḥanīfah, precede all other works written by Hanafi jurists down the ages.

The works of Shaybānī, other than those of *Zahir al-Riwayah,* have been classified above into two categories. Works mentioned under 'B' have been published and are generally available. Of these, *Ziyādāt al- Ziyadat,* is a kind of appendix or complementary volume of *Ziyadat,* and some scholars have considered it to be a part of *Ziyādāt* and hence it may also be included in category 'A'.

Muwatta' and *Kitāb al-Athar* are the two books which were compiled by Shaybānī mainly as collections of traditions. Shaybānī's *Muwatta'* is one of the more popular versions of the work that go by that name. Shaybānī had spent almost three years with Malik and had studied Hadith under him and other traditionists of Madinah. As a result of his stay with Malik, he was able to prepare his own version of the *Muwatta'*, which is different in several respects from that of Yahya ibn Yahya al- Masmudī: it records the opinions of the Iraqi jurists on different issues after narrating the *ahadith* which he reports from Malik. It also refers to the sources from where the Iraqi jurists draw their opinions. It also records the attitude of the Iraqi jurists towards the admissibility or otherwise of the narrations mentioned in the *Muwatta'*. Contrary to the practice of his Spanish counterpart, Shaybānī does not refer to the opinions and rulings of Malik on many legal issues. Darqutni, in his treatise on the twenty-two versions of the *Muwatta'*, has considered Shaybānī's as one of the best.

The total number of *aḥadīth* and other narratives in Shaybānī's version of Muwatta' is one thousand, almost all of which have been narrated from Malik except some 175 traditions which have been taken by Shaybānī from other, mostly Madinan, authorities. The popularity of Shaybānī's *Muwatta'* has, in the main, been confined to the Central and South Asian countries. However, it also had some recognition in Muslim Spain.

Kitab al-Athār is an independent work of the traditions collected by Shaybānī and is mostly based on the narratives coming down to him from Abū Ḥanīfah. Apart from Abū Ḥanīfah, there are some twenty other scholars whose narratives have been included in Kitab al-Athar, although the number of traditions so collected is limited. Most of the traditions, whether they go back directly to the Prophet (peace be on him) or only to a Companion or to a Successor, have been transmitted by Ibrahim al-Nakha'i, the intellectual father of all Iraqi jurists.

But the most important work of Shaybānī, which prominently reflects his genius as a great jurist, is his *Kitab al-Hujjah 'ala ahl al-Madinah*, perhaps the best example of legal reasoning in the second century. The book, as its title indicates, supports the legal doctrines of the Iraqi jurists as against those of the Madīnan school. It is said that the book left a deep impression on the thinking and style of Shafi'ī. In his Kitab al-Umm, wherever Shafi'ī offers a critique of other legal doctrines, especially those of Malik, he seems to have been influenced by the style and mode of argumentation of Shaybānī in *Kitab al-Hujjah.*

Some historians of Hanafi jurisprudence have gone even further. They have pointed to Shaybānī's influence on the development of Malikī jurisprudence through Asad ibn Furat, a disciple of both Shaybānī and Malik and the author of the well-known work *al-Asadiyyah* which became one of the major sources of Malikī jurisprudence in North Africa and Spain. Asad ibn Furat had settled down in Qayrawan, where a large number of students studied under him. Saḥnun, the compiler and editor of *al-Mudawwanah*, the main source of the Maliki legal doctrines, was one of them.

Asad ibn Furat is reported to have been advised by Malik himself to go to Iraq to quench his thirst for legal knowledge. Asad, accordingly, went to Iraq where his extraordinary legal mind found satisfaction in the circles of Abu Yusuf and Shaybānī. He was especially attracted to the circle of Shaybānī, who not only accorded him special treatment but also provided him with financial support." It was after completing his studies and research under Shaybānī that he wrote *al-Asadiyyah* and transmitted Shaybānī's methodology to his Maghribi students, including Sahnun in Qayrawan. Asad wrote some sixty books and treatises on various aspects of law, embodying the rulings of Malik and his Maghribi disciples, which bear the imprint of the style of his Iraqi teacher.

The remaining works of Shaybānī have mostly failed to reach us except for some fragments from a couple of them. Out of these, *al-Makhārij fi'l-Hiyal* has been edited and published. It mostly deals with a novel aspect of the law, namely the legal devices for which the Hanafis became known since the very beginning of their legal school.

Like many other jurists of his time, Shaybānī employs a dialogue form in some of his writings, especially when he compares his arguments with those of other jurists. This form not only keeps the discussion lively but also greatly helps the reader, in most cases, to follow the line of argument adopted by the jurist concerned.

(VIII)

Although Shaybānī was not the first jurist to write on *Siyar,* he was undoubtedly the most prolific writer on the subject among the early jurists. All his contemporaries, senior as well as junior, lagged far behind him as far as the quantum of writings on *Siyar* is concerned. In this respect only his disciple and junior contemporary, Shafi'ī, follow him more closely than others. Apart from dealing extensively with the subject in several of his legal works, Shaybānī devoted two independent books exclusively to the exposition of Muslim *International Law* as expounded by his master, Abū Ḥanīfah.

As already mentioned, he prepared his *Kitab al-Siyar al-Saghir*, or the Shorter Book on *International Law*, not long after the demise of Abū Ḥanīfah. This work was completed under the guidance and supervision of his erstwhile colleague-cum-teacher, Abu Yusuf, who approved its final draft when it was submitted to him on completion. According to Khadduri, it was this shorter work which was known as the *Siyar* of Abū Ḥanīfah because it contains mostly the opinions of Abū Hanifah on questions pertaining to the interaction of Muslims with others at the international level, and it was this very book to which Awza'i had written a rejoinder. But Khadduri's remarks on the subject seem to be mutually contradictory. He denies the popular contention that Shaybānī had written this book before 157 AH in which case this cannot be considered to be the *Siyar* of Abū Ḥanīfah of which Awza'ī wrote a refutation. He also conjectures that the *Siyar* attributed to Abū Hanifah might have been written by Abu Yusuf and might not have reached us. On the other hand, Khadduri declares a chapter from Shaybānī's *Kitab al-Asl* as his *Siyar* and embarks upon its translation without even perhaps trying to check whether the real *al-Siyar al-Saghir* was in existence or not.

What seems to be plausible is that the lectures of Abū Ḥanīfah on *Siyar*, which were recorded and preserved by his students, became known as the *Siyar* of Abū Ḥanīfah and reached the Syrian jurist who was tempted to write a rejoinder, of which Abu Yusuf subsequently took note. *Shaybānī's al-Siyar al-Saghir* also seems to have played a role in that controversy.

However, the adverse remark of the Syrian jurist prompted Shaybānī to write a more detailed and comprehensive book on the subject. It seems that Awza'i's remark kept on irritating him, and he was eventually able to find time. during the later part of his life. to write his *magnum opus* on the subject, namely, *Kitab al-Siyar al-Kabir*.

This was perhaps his last book and was greatly acclaimed by the academics and jurists of his time.

Shaybānī got a special copy of the book prepared and sent it to the Caliph Harun al-Rashid. The Caliph accepted the precious gift with gratitude and considered it one of the most prestigious accomplishments of his reign. He asked his sons Amin and Ma'mun to attend the lectures of Shaybānī and to study the book under him. Both attended his classes and took notes of his lectures on the subject.

The book acquired much popularity especially in the Hanafi circles, and was taught as an advanced textbook on the subject. It was commented upon by various scholars, the most famous being *al-Sarakhsī,* the well-known commentator on the summary of Shaybānī's *Zahir al-Riwayah.* He dictated the greater part of his commentary from the same prison hole in Awzjand. It seems that Sarakhsī did not possess any notes while he was dictating his commentary. It is not clear whether he possessed any copy of *al-Siyar al-Kabir* or not. In case he did not possess a copy of the text, it is difficult to determine how much of the original he was able to incorporate in his commentary by dint of his extraordinary memory, even though that was something not unusual among the Muslim scholars of the early centuries of Islam. However, it may well be probable that the students sitting around the pit possessed copies of the original and read out to the imprisoned teacher the passages of the original, which Sarakhsī set out to elaborate and explain. Recitation of the text by the students in order that it be explained by the teacher was, and still is, a prevalent practice in the traditional centres of Islamic learning.

Al-Siyar al-Kabir was also translated into Turkish by a Turkish jurist, Muhammad Munib Ayntābi, who wrote a short commentary on it. The short commentary has not yet been published and is preserved in manuscript form in the well-known library of Shaykh al-Islam Arif Hikmat in Madinah. The Turkish translation was published long ago, in 1240 AH 1825 CE, in Istanbul on the orders of Sultan Mahmud Khan to serve as a source of guidance for the Ottoman army in its relations with other armies in times of war and peace.

Unfortunately, the original text of *al-Siyar al-Kabir* in its original form has not reached us: it has only come down to us along with the commentary of Sarakhsī. The text and the commentary are so interwoven that it is extremely difficult to separate the two. Any effort to distinguish the two is bound to be arbitrary. The editors of the Hyderabad edition of the commentary have tried to identify the text by placing it in parentheses. However, their identification is different in several places from the text identified by *Salah al-Din al-Munajjid*. However, in spite of the conjectural nature of the text identification by the learned editors of the two editions, the text can be distinguished with a fairly high degree of certitude in most cases.

The contribution of Shaybānī in the systematization and codification of the *International Law* of Islam has invited the attention of a number of Western scholars. After the publication of the Turkish translation of the book as early as 1825, the famous Austrian historian Hammer Purgstall was so impressed by Shaybānī's work that he conferred on him the title of the Hugo Grotius of the Muslims. Hans Kruse has also referred to this honour bestowed on Shaybānī by the Austrian historian may, however, be pointed out that Shaybānī (d. 804 CE) lived more than eight hundred years before Grotius (d. 1645 CE). If at all any title is to be awarded to either of the two, then it is not Shaybānī who should be called the Hugo Grotius of the Muslim East, rather it is Grotius who deserves to be honoured with the title of the Shaybānī of the Christian West.

Hans Kruse, on his part, renewed the effort to introduce Shaybānī to Western scholars. Earlier, he had produced some research papers to highlight Shaybānī's contribution to *International Law*. In 1955, he founded an organization known as the Shaybānī Society of *International Law*. However, either this society failed to attract the attention of scholars or Hans Kruse himself was unable to pursue his efforts further.

(IX)

Kitab al-Siyar al Saghir was generally believed to be extinct. Modern writers on Shaybānī's contribution-Kawthari, Hamidullah and Khadduri make no mention of the existence of the book. In his effort to make his readers believe that both the *Siyar*s of Shaybānī had been lost, Khadduri arbitrarily picks up a chapter from *Kitab al-Asl* and presents it as Shaybānī's *Siyar*. The material included by him in this book does contain Shaybānī's ideas on the *Siyar*, but it can in no case be called *al-Siyar al-Saghir* of Shayban or Shaybānī's *Siyar*.

As we have pointed out earlier, al-Hakim al-Shahid Muhammad ibn Muhammad al-Marwazi had prepared a summary of Shaybānī's six books of *Zahir al-Riwayah* which included his two works on *Siyar* as well. In this summary, Hakim had adopted the entire text of *al-Siyar al-Saghir* of Shaybānī in the original form instead of attempting to make his own summary of the two *Siyars*.

This assertion has not only been verified by its most popular and authoritative commentator, al-Sarakhsī, but is also supported by the fact that most of the extant manuscripts of *al-Kafl* use the title *al-Siyar al-Saghir* for the relevant chapter in *al-Kafl.* A brief note on the manuscripts has been added at the beginning of the Arabic text.

(X)

The information given above about the writings of Shaybānī on *Siyar* is based on the data preserved by biographers and chroniclers. They are of the view that Shaybānī wrote only two books on *Siyar,* as mentioned above. However, the present writer has been able to discover a third work attributed to Shayban on *International Law,* which is preserved (under No. 1156 of the Arabic manuscripts) in the Laleli Library of Istanbul, now transferred among some 113 other collections to the Sulemaniye library. The work is titled *al-Mukhtar min al-Siyar al-Kabir,* attributed to the "*Imam*... son of *Imam* Muhammad ibn al-Hasan al- Shaybānī". An old calligrapher has written on the title page: "This is the last book of *Imam* Muhammad, and he did not give it any name." Likewise, on the last page (fo1.87), another calligrapher has also indicated that the book had been authored by "... [titles]... Abu 'Abd Allah Muḥammad ibn al-Hasan, a disciple of... Abū Ḥanīfah... Another indication of the book being the work of Shaybānī is the chain of narrators proceeding the traditions mentioned in the first chapter of the book. Like his *al-Siyar al-Kabir,* this new *Siyar* was also compiled by Isma'il ibn Tawbah al-Qazwini and Abū Sulayman al-Juzānī, the two prominent disciples of Shaybānī. Likewise, the initial chains of narrators of the two *Siyars* are also common, namely, Shams'i-

A'immah al- Halawānī from Qādī Abu'l-Hasayn ibn al-Khadir al-Nasafi from Abú Bakr Muhammad ibn al-*Fadl* and Abū Ishaq Ibrahim ibn Muhammad both from 'Abd Allah ibn Muhammad al-Harithi from Abu Muhammad 'Abd al-Rahim al-Sammānī from Abū Ibāhīm Ismail ibn Tawbah al- Qazwīnī from Muhammad ibn al-Hasan al-Shaybānī. Moreover, there are two more writings on the title page (in somewhat bad handwriting) attributing the book to Shaybānī.

The title of the book suggests that it is primarily a summary of Shaybānī's own al-*Siyar* al-al-Kabir, presumably prepared by himself. As against a total of 218 chapters in *al-Siyar al-Kabir*, there are only 37 chapters in al-Mukhtar. Out of these 37 chapters, 34 are found in the first volume of *Sharh al-Siyar al-Kabir*. It means that either the Mukhtar represents a summary of only the first part of *al-Siyar al-Kabir*, or the resent manuscript is incomplete, of which, however, there is no indication at least in the extant manuscript.

The date of the manuscript is not known. However, there are inscriptions and seals of Sultan Salim Khan ibn Sultan Mustafa Khan dated 1217 AH (i.e. 1803 CE).

NOTES AND REFERENCES

1. See. 33, 34 below. Other scholars have also dealt with this question. For some such views, see L.N. Tandon and S.K. Kapoor, *International Law* (Lahore, 1980), pp. 33 ff. Some scholars have preferred to call it 'positive international morality'. See *Ibid.*, p. 44.
2. This controversy finds mention in almost all the classical books on English jurisprudence; see, for example, Salmond,

Jurisprudence (London, 1966), pp. 54-57; G.W. Paton, A Textbook of *Jurisprudence* (Oxford, 1954), pp. 78-83.

3. Tandon and Kapoor, *International Law*, p. 34.
4. Majid Khadduri, The Islamic Law of Nations: Shaybānī's Sale (Baltimore, Johns Hopkins Press, 1966), p. xii.
5. The principle of reciprocity was recognized by Muslim jurists from the very beginning. As early as the days of the Caliph Umar, the principle was applied to lay down rules of law and principles of policy. The imposition of customs duty on non-Muslim traders entering the Territory of Islam on the basis of reciprocity is a classic example. See, for a detailed elaboration of the law on this subject, among others Ibn Nujaym, *al-Bahr al-Ra'iq*, (Beirut, n.d.), vol. II, pp. 248-251. For a brief modern exposition, see Wahbah al-Zuhayli, *al-Fiqh al-Islami wa Adillatuh* (Damascus, 1989), vol. II, pp. 825-826.
6. Cf. Muhammad Hamidullah, *The Muslim Conduct of State* (Lahore, 1973), p. 34, 125, 138, 151-52, 166.
7. See, for example. Khadduri, *Ibid*, p. 5.
8. It has been held predominantly by the jurists and the commentators of the Qur'an that the instructions to fight till the end or till the non-Muslims are subjugated and forced to pay *jizyah* was applicable only to the infidels of Arabia, and their application may not be extended to other non-Muslims. See, for an elaborate discussion, *Amin Ahsan Islahi*, *Tadabbur-i Qur'an* (Lahore, 1983), vol. III, pp 523-27, 536-546.
9. Abu'l-Wafa' al-Afghafi, "Introduction" to Abu Yusuf, *al-Radd 'ala Siyar al-Awza'i* (Cairo, n.d.). p. 2. Cf. Zafar Ishaq Ansari, "An Early Discussion on Islamic Jurisprudence: Some Notes on *al-Radd ala Siyar al-Awza'i,* in Khurshid Ahmad and Zafar Ishaq Ansari (eds.), Islamic Perspectives (Leicester and Jeddah, 1979), pp. 148-49.

10. 10. Ibrahim al-Fazari, *Kitab al-Siyar*, edited by Faruq Ḥamudah, (Beruit, 1987), pp. 432. See also Khadduri, *Ibid* and Hamidullah, *Muslim Conduct of State*, p. 62.
11. Amir Shakib Arsalan, (ed.), *Mahasin al- Masa'i fi Manaqib al- Imam al- Awza'i* (Cairo, n.d.), pp. 13-14, nn.
12. Al-Afghani, "Introduction", p. 2.
13. Sarakhsi, *Sharh al- Siyar al- Kabir*, ed. Salah al- *Din* al- Munajjid (Cairo, 1971), p. 3.
14. Afghafi, "Introduction", p. 3.
15. Abu Yusuf, *al- Radd 'ala Siyar al- Awza'i* (Cairo, n.d.), pp. 80-83.
16. *Ibid.* p. 94; Cf. Ṭabarī, *Ikhtilaf al- Fuqaha'*, ed. Joseph Schacht (Berlin, 1933), pp. 56-57.
17. Abu Yusuf, al Radd, pp. 96-98; cf. al- Jaṣṣās, Ahkam al- Qur'an vol. I, p. 471; Sarakhsī, *al-mabsut*, vol. XIV, p. 59.
18. Abu Yusuf, *al-Radd*, p. 98 ff. For a penetrating study of the book see Zafar Ishaq Ansari, "An Early Discussion", op. cit., pp. 147-67.
19. See, for example, al- Radd, pp. 68-70, 77-78.
20. See, for example, *Ibid.*, pp. 68-70, 77-78.
21. *Ibid.* pp. 5-12.
22. *Ibid.* pp. 17-22, 40 ff.
23. *Ibid.* pp. 37-40.
24. *Ibid.* p. 66 (Qur'an 48:25).
25. *Ibid.* pp. 65-68.
26. *Ibid.* pp. 80-83.
27. *Ibid.* pp. 96-98.
28. *Ibid.* pp. 99-103.
29. Shafi'ī, *Kitab al-Umm* (Beirut, 1973), vol. IV, pp. 260-293.
30. Ṭabarī, *Ikhtilaf al-Fuqaha'*, pp. 11, 37, 180, 212.
31. Published in Berlin in 1933 with a German introduction by the editor, Joseph Schacht.

32. Hobbes, Pufendorf and Bentham are among the earliest authorities to deny the legal character of the law of nations. Later, Austin also took up the same position. See Oppenheim, *International Law* (London, 1955), vol. I, pp. 7-8; see also John Austin, Lectures on *Jurisprudence* (London, 1873), vol. I, pp. 187-88.
33. This was contended by the celebrated English jurist of the nineteenth century, John Austin, who described *International Law* as something analogous to the rules binding a club or society. He used to call the rules of *International Law* as merely opinions and sentiments. See his Lectures on Jurisprudence, vol. 1, pp. 187-88, 222.
34. See for further details, J.G. Starke, An Introduction to *International Law* (London, 1972), pp. 18-22; and Tandon and Kapoor, *International Law*, pp. 48-49, 51-56.
35. Oppenheim concedes that the Modern Law of Nations is a product of Christian civilization. According to him, it originally arose among the states of Christendom only and for hundreds of years, was confined to those states. See Oppenheim, *International Law*, pp. 48-49, 51-56.
36. Cf. Khadduri, op. cit., pp. 2-3.
37. See, for example, Oppenheim, *International Law*, pp. 84-88.
38. See for a brief discussion on Kelsenian exposition of the individuals as subjects of *International Law*, Starke, *International Law*, pp. 63-66.
39. For such a case, where non-Muslims invoked the rules of the *International Law* of Islam to secure the vacation of the city of Samarqand by the conquering Muslim army see Baladhuri, *Futuḥ al-Buldan*, p. 428. The rights and privileges of the *Harbi* have been

explicitly discussed by Muslim jurists. See Muhammad Haidullah, Muslim Conduct of State, pp. 202-204.

40. Cf. Khadduri, op. cit., p. 2.
41. Oppenheim, *International Law*, pp. 48-49.
42. Even as late as 1844, a German scholar considered Christian morality to be essential to the highest law of humanity. See Hans Kruse, "*The Foundations of Islamic International Jurisprudence*", Journal of Pakistan Historical Society (October 1955), pp. 232-33.
43. See, for various examples of the application of this principle, Sarakhsi, *Sharh al-Siyar al- Kabir*, vol. IV, pp. 283, 284, 285, 286.
44. Muhammad Zahid al- Kawthari, Bulagh al- Amani *fi Sirat al- Imam Muhammad ibn al- Hasan al- Shaybānī* (Hims, 1969), pp. 5-6.
45. *Ibid.* pp. 7-9
46. Al-Khatib al- Baghdadi, Ta'rikh Baghdad (Cairo, 1931), vol. II, pp. 174-175.
47. Al- Kawthari, Bulugh, pp. 9-11.
48. Şaymari, Akhbar Abi Hanifah (Lahore), pp. 123-24.
49. *Ibid.* p. 123.
50. *Ibid.*
51. *Ibid.* 50.
52. Kawthari, Bulugh, pp. 53-54; Saymarī, Press, p. 121
53. Kawthari, Bulugh, p. 90.
54. Works given under (xviii) to (xxii) have been mentioned by Ibn al-Nadim and *al-Fihrist.*
55. It may be noted that this last-mentioned work on *Usul al-Fiqh* predates Shafi'ī's *Risalah.*
56. Cf. Ibn Abidin, Rasa'il Ibn 'Abidin, vol. 1, pp. 16-19.
57. Cf. Kawthari, Bulugh, p. 78.
58. *Ibid.*
59. *Ibid.* p. 79.

60. *Ibid.*
61. The only edition of *al-Nafi al-Kabir* was published in Lucknow in 1291 AH. The author has referred to some other commentaries of the book (pp. 18-24).
62. Kawthari and Bulagh, pp. 79-80, have quoted some such statements.
63. *Ibid.*
64. See for details Fuat Sezgin, History of Arabic Literature (Leiden, 1967), vol. I, pp. 421-33.
65. Kawthari, Bulugh, p. 77
66. Kitab al-Asl is also known as al-Mabsut. It has now been edited by Abul-Wafa al-Afghani and has been recently reprinted in Karachi (n.d.) in five volumes.
67. For some discussion on the peculiarities of Shaybānī's version of the *Muwatta'*, see *'Abd al-Hayy Lakhnawi, al-Ta'liq al- Mumajjad,* (Lucknow, 1925), pp. 26-27. It may be pointed out that Lakhnawi prefers the Shaybānī version to that of Yahya ibn Yahyā.
68. Quoted by Kawthari, Bulugh, pp. 11-12.
69. *Ibid.* p. 83.
70. *Ibid.* p. 85.
71. Kawthari (*Ibid.* p. 77) is of the view that Shafi'ī's style and methodology were influenced by *Kitab al-Asl* rather than by his *Kitab al-Hujjah* as against the view preferred by the present writer.
72. See for example, Kawthari, Bulugh, pp. 107-1 16 ff.
73. *Ibid.* pp. 17- 18
74. Published in Leipzig, 1930, ed. by Joseph Schacht; reprinted in Baghdad, n.d.

75. Cf. Bukhari's criticism, rather attack, on Abū Ḥanīfah's alleged views about the Hiyal in his al-Jami' al-Sahih, Kitab al-Hiyal; see also Ibn Hajar, Fath al-Bari. (Beirut, 1985), vol. XII, pp. 274-294.
76. Khadduri, op. cit., p. 41, also f.n. 97.
77. Hans Kruse, "The Foundation of Islamic International Jurisprudence", Journal of the Pakistan Historical Society (October, 1955), p. 240.
78. *Ibid.*, p. 238; see also Salah al-*Din* Munajjid's Introduction to *al-Kabir's Sharh* (Cairo, 1957), vol. I, p. 14.
79. Kawthari, Bulugh, p. 81. The commentary is entitled: *Tafsir al-Masir ft Sharh Kitab al-Siyar al-Kabir*. See the catalogue of Tapkapi Seray (Istanbul, 1964), pp. 381-382.
80. Kawthari, Bulugh.
81. *Al- Munajjid*, Introduction, pp. 15-16.
82. (Hyderabad, 1335 AH), four volumes.
83. The present writer has compared the first volumes of the two editions in this respect. The difference between the texts of the two does not seem to be less than fifteen to twenty per cent.
84. Hans Kruse, "*al-Shaybānī on International Instruments*", Journal of Pakistan Historical Society, vol. I (1953), p. 91.
85. *Ibid.*
86. Khadduri, op. cit., pp. 56-57.
87. *Ibid*, pp. 41-42.
88. Sarakhsi, *al-mabsut*, vol. X, p. 144: "[Here] ends the commentary of *al-Siyar al-Saghir* comprising valuable views dictated by the one who speaks for the luminous truth, who is imprisoned for its cause, who is detained and is waiting for his release by the All-Knowing, the All-Powerful."
89. I have consulted the following manuscripts of *al-Kafl* for establishing the text of *al-Siyar al-Saghir*:

(i) Original Manuscript in Hajji Bashir Agha Library, no. 288, pp. 101-1 119- b-126- b.

(ii) Feyzullah Library, no. 923, pp. 101-1 122- b-141- b.

(iii) Hamidiye Library, no. 545, pp. 101-1 92- b-99- b.

(iv) Carullah Library, no. 820, pp. 101-1 141- b-148- a.

(v) Sehid Ali Pass Library, no. 912, pp. 101-1 145- b-153- b.

(vi) Ayasofya Library, no. 1362, pp. 1362-1 139- b-145- b.

(vii) Ayasofya Library, no. 1363, pp. 1363-1 127- a-133- a.

(viii) Damad Ibrahim Library, no. 646, pp. 101-1 194- b-203.

(ix) Feyzullah Library, no. 922, pp. 101-1 207- b-217- b.

(x) Sulaymaniye Library, no. 580, pp. 188-a-198-b.

(xi) Atif Afindi Library, no. 1005, pp. 157-a-163-a.

90. Cf. *al-Mukhtar*, folio 1- b, and Sharh al- Siyar al-Kabir, ed. Salah 'l-*Din* al- Munajjid, reprint Afghanistan, 1405, Vol. I, p. 5.

91. *Sharh al- Siyar al- Kabir*, op. cit., pp. 406-408.

****

The Shorter book On International Muslim Law

Chapter I : Instructions of the Prophet about the Conduct of War and International Relations

1. Muhammad [ibn al-Hasan al-Shaybānī] narrates from Abū Ḥanīfah, on the authority of 'Alqamah ibn Marthad, from 'Abd Allah ibn Buraydah, from his father [Buraydah] who reports: "Whenever the Messenger of Allah, peace be on him, sent an army or a group of troops he used to admonish its leader to fear Allah in his personal behaviour and to be pleasant to the Muslims who accompanied him". Then he would say: "Fight in the name of Allah and in the way of Allah; fight only those who disbelieve in Allah. Do not misappropriate; do not commit treachery; do not mutilate [the dead]; and do not kill a child. When you meet the polytheists who are your enemy, invite them to Islam. If they accept Islam, accept it from them and hold yourselves back from them. Then, invite them to move over from their territory to the territory of *Muhajirin.* If they do that, accept it from them and hold yourselves back from them. In case they do not, tell them that they are like other non-resident Muslims: they shall be subject to the injunctions of Allah applicable to other Muslims; however, they shall have no share in the *fay* of the state or the spoils of war. If they refuse [to accept Islam], invite them to pay *jizyah.* If they do that, accept it from them and hold yourselves back from them. When you lay siege to the people of a fort or a city, and they ask you to allow them to surrender, subject to the commandment of Allah, do not [commit yourselves to] do that because you might not know what is the commandment of Allah regarding them. Rather, bring them to the acceptance of your own decision, and then decide about them according to your own opinion. When you lay siege to the people of a fort or a city, and they

ask you to grant them the guarantee of Allah and the guarantee of His Messenger, do not give them the guarantee of Allah or the guarantee of Messenger; rather, grant them your own guarantee and the guarantee of your forefathers for it is less grave if you were to fail to fulfil your guarantee and your forefathers' guarantee.

2. Ibn 'Abbas reports that *khums* (one-fifth of the war booty) was divided during the days of the Messenger of Allah (peace be on him) into five shares: one share for Allah and His Messenger, one share for the kith and kin [of the Prophet], one share for the destitute (*masakin*); one share for the orphans; and one share for the wayfarer. He [Ibn 'Abbas] said: "Thereafter Abu Bakr, 'Umar, 'Uthman and 'Ali (may Allah be pleased with them) divided it into three shares: one for the orphans, one for the destitute (*masakin*) and one for the wayfarers".

3. It is reported that Abu Ja'far Muhammad ibn 'Ali said that 'Ali held the same view about *khums* as was held by his family members. But he disliked acting contrary to the views of Abu Bakr and 'Umar.

4. It is reported that Ibn 'Abbas (may Allah be pleased with them) said that 'Umar offered to us that we may arrange for the marriage of our unmarried persons out of khums and pay our debts out of it. We refused to accept this and insisted that it should be handed over to us, and he [i.e.,,, 'Umar] refused to do so.

5. It has been reported that Sa'id ibn al-Musayyab has said that the Messenger of Allah (peace be on him) distributed the *khums* on the day of the conquest of Khaybar. He distributed the share of the kith and kin among Banu Hashim and Banu 'l-Muttalib. 'Uthman ibn 'Affan and Jubayr ibn Mut'im spoke to the Messenger of Allah (peace be on him) about this. They said: "We and Banu'l- Muttalib are

equally related to you in kinship and lineage, but you have given them and excluded us!" The Messenger of Allah (peace be on him) said, "We and Banu'l- Muttalib have always been together, in the days of the Ignorance' as well as in Islam".

6. It is reported that Jabir ibn 'Abd Allah said: "*Khums* was used to provide riding animals [to the persons going for *Jihad*] in the way of Allah. It was also spent on the emergencies faced by the people. But when wealth increased, it was also spent on other things".

7. It is reported by Ibn Abbas that a man found his lost camel in the booty; polytheists earlier captured this camel. He asked the Messenger of Allah (peace be on him) about it. He answered: "If you found it before the booty was distributed, it is yours, but if you found it after the booty had been distributed, you may take it by paying its price if you wish".

8. It is reported from Sha'bi that 'Umar ibn al-Khattab had declared the people of Sawad to be the People of *Dhimmah.*

9. It is reported from Ata' that Najdah wrote to Ibn 'Abbas to enquire whether a slave had any share in the booty. [He also enquired]: "Did women use to join the Messenger of Allah (peace be on him) in the battles? When does a child become entitled to a share in the booty? What is the share of the kith and kin (*Dhawi'l- Qurba*)? In reply, Ibn Abbas wrote to him: "A slave has no right to receive any share from the booty; rather he will be given something by way of gift; that women used to accompany the Messenger of Allah (peace be on him) to nurse the wounded, and that they were [also] given something by way of gift; and that a child has no right to receive any share from the booty until he attains puberty. As to the share of the kith and kin (*Dhawi'l- Qurba*), he wrote that 'Umar had offered to us that we could

arrange for the marriage of the unmarried among us out of that share, and pay our debts from it. But we refused to accept this arrangement and insisted that he should hand it over to us. But 'Umar refused to do so”.

10. It is reported from 'Umar that he said: "A slave has no right to receive any share from the booty".

11. It is reported from Ibn 'Abbas that the Messenger of Allah (peace be on him) distributed Badr's booty after he returned to Madinah.

12. It is reported from Muhammad ibn Ishaq and al-Kalbi that the Messenger of Allah (peace be on him) distributed the booty of the battle of Hunayn at Ji'iranah after his return from Ta'if. As to Khaybar, he had already conquered its land, and his writ was already being enforced in it; therefore, the distribution of the booty there was just like its distribution in Madinah. The Messenger of Allah (peace be on him) distributed the booty there before he left the place. He distributed the spoils of the Banu'l-Mustaliq in their own territory, which he had conquered.

13. It is reported from Ibn 'Abbas that the Messenger of Allah (peace be on him) gave one share to the foot-soldier and two shares to the horseman on the day of Badr.

14. It is reported from Dahhak that Abu Bakr al-Siddiq consulted the Muslims about the share of the kith and kin (*Dhawi'l-Qurba*). They were of the opinion that it may [now] be allocated for the [expenses incurred on] cavalry and weaponry.

15. It is reported from Ibn 'Abbas about the grant made by the person who does not go for *jihad* to him who goes for it," that he

said: "If it is spent on the mount and weaponry there is no harm; but if it is spent on household effects, there is no good in it".

16. It is reported from 'Umar ibn al-Khattab (may Allah be pleased with him), that he used to dispatch the bachelor, rather than the married person, to take part in fighting; he also used to give the horses of those who did not go for *jihad* to those who took part in it.

17. It is reported from Jarir ibn 'Abd Allah that Mu'awiyah once imposed a special military tax on the people of Kufah and exempted Jarir and his children from it; upon this, Jarir said: "We shall not accept it, but we will make some of our wealth available to the warriors".

18. It is reported from Abū Marzuq about a gentleman from amongst the Companions of the Messenger of Allah (peace be on him) that he conquered a village in Morocco. Then he addressed his colleagues and said in the course of the address: "I will only tell you what I have heard from the Messenger of Allah (peace be on him). I heard him say on the day of the conquest of Khaybar:" Whosoever believes in Allah and the Last Day he should not irrigate other's crops with his water. Items of the booty should not be sold before they are distributed. No beast out of the *fay* of the Muslims should be mounted upon to be returned to the public exchequer only after it has been emaciated. No cloth from the *fay* of the Muslims should be worn to be returned only after becoming shabby.

19. It is reported from al-Hasan that the Messenger of Allah (peace be on him) had prohibited the killing of women.

20. It is reported from Ibn Sirin that he said: "The Messenger of Allah (peace be on him) used to have a choice of his own from the booty

which he used to select exclusively for himself before the distribution of the booty: a sword, or a horse, or a coat of arm or any such thing".

21. It is reported by Ibn Abbas that a man from amongst the polytheists fell into the ditch and died. Muslims were offered some money in consideration of his corpse. They enquired from the Messenger of Allah (peace be on him) about it, but he forbade them [to accept that money].

22. It is reported from Sha'bi and Ziyadah ibn 'Alaqah that 'Umar ibn al-Khattab wrote to Saad ibn Abi Waqqas: "I am reinforcing you with a group of Syrian people. If someone from amongst them joins you before the dead bodies get decomposed give them their share from the booty".

23. It is reported from Abu Qasit who says that Abu Bakr al-Siddiq (may Allah be pleased with him) sent 'Ikrimah ibn Abi Jahl at the head of five hundred men as a reinforcement to Ziyad ibn Labid al-Bayadi and al-Muhajir ibn Umayyah al-Makhzümi to Yemen. They reached there when the latter had already conquered Nujayr. He [Abu Qasit] reports that Abu Bakr gave them a share of the booty.

24. It is reported by Ibn 'Abbas that the Messenger of Allah (peace be on him) received help from the Jews of the tribe of Banu Qaynuqa against the tribe of Banu Qarayzah. But he did not give them anything from the booty.

25. It is reported from Daḥhak that the Messenger of Allah (peace be on him) came out on the day of Uhud; suddenly, he saw a wonderful battalion. He asked, "Who are they?" The people answered: "The

Jews of such-and-such tribe". He said: "We do not seek help from the disbelievers".

26. It is reported from al-Hakam that Abu Bakr wrote to him about a Roman prisoner. He had written: "Do not accept any ransom for him even though you are offered two kilograms of gold. But either you should execute him, or he should embrace Islam".

27. It is reported from al-Hasan and 'Ata' that they said about the prisoner of war: "He should not be executed; rather, he should either be ransomed or set free as an act of kindness [without any ransom]". But Abu Yusuf says that the opinion of al-Hasan and 'Ata' in this matter is nothing.

28. It is reported from 'Abd Allah ibn Awfa that he said: "The food items acquired in Khaybar were not distributed in five shares; it was only a meagre quantity. Whenever some of us needed something, he would take according to his need".

29. It is reported from 'Abd Allah ibn 'Amr who says that the Messenger of Allah (peace be on him) said: "Muslims are one hand against all others; their blood is equal unto each other; even their junior- most has an obligation to honour their guarantee.

30. It is reported from Ibn 'Abbas that he said: "The Messenger of Allah (peace be on him) started fighting in the month of Muharram, on the first day of the month. He stayed there for forty days and finally conquered it [i.e., Ta'if] in the month of Safar".

Section: Prohibition of warlike operations during the sacred months has been abrogated

31. It is reported from Mujahid that he says that the prohibition of war in the sacred months has been abrogated. The abrogating verse is the saying of Allah: "Then slay the polytheists wherever you find them...' (Qur'an 9:5), which has abrogated the verse: "And they ask you concerning the Sacred Month and the war during it. Say war in it is grave..." (Qur'an 2:217). This is also the opinion of Abū Ḥanīfah and Abu Yusuf. On the other hand, Kalbi used to say: "This [prohibition] has not been abrogated". But we do not take the view of Kalbi.

Chapter II : The army's treatment of the Disbelievers

32. When the [Muslim] army fights against a country where the message of Islam has already reached, it is good if they are again invited [to accept Islam]. But if that is not done, even then, there is no harm. If an ambush is made against them [i.e., disbelievers] in the daytime or during the night without [formally] inviting them [to Islam], it makes no difference. There is no harm if they [i.e., the Muslims] demolish their castles and flood them. They should not divide the spoils of war while they are still in the Territory of War until they take it to the Territory of Islam and acquire full possession of it. However, if the acquisitions of war are distributed there [i.e., in the territory of the war], it is also allowed. Abū Yusuf says: "If the Government does not find any transport to carry them, they may be distributed while they are still in the Territory of War. This we have found in some of the versions of this book".

33. If there is some food or fodder in the booty and someone needs it, he may take from it according to his need. Likewise, he can take something from the weaponry of the booty if he needs it for fighting, but he should return it to the booty as soon as his need is over. But it is not proper to do so without need.

34. After this, he [i.e., Shaybānī] says: "If the enemy hits him with an arrow and he hits them back with it or snatches a sword from someone from amongst the enemy and strikes with it, there is no harm in it. As to the chattel, the garments and the cattle, it is not proper to derive any benefit from them before distribution. If they are in need of these things even, then it is not proper to distribute them in the Territory of War. However, if someone stands in need of

these things to the extent that he fears his death, then there is no harm if these are used even before the distribution.

35. However, the captives should not be distributed among the warriors, even though people need them until these are taken to the Territory of Islam. These [i.e., the captives] should not be sold there; they should rather be asked to travel, if they can, to the Territory of Islam. If they are not able to travel and the Muslim Commander does not have additional transport and none from amongst the [Muslim] army voluntarily agrees to provide them transport, in that case, the males should be executed, and the women and children should be left behind. No one having additional transport shall be forced to carry the booty with him. As to the weaponry and the chattel, it should be put on fire if it is not possible to carry them to the Territory of Islam. As to the cattle and the animals, if these have already been gathered together, these should neither be dispersed nor mutilated but should be killed and burnt so that the infidels may not be able to derive any benefit from them.

36. He [Shaybānī] saw no harm in the demolition of the villages of the Territory of War which came their way. As to the land of the enemy captured by them [i.e.,,, the Muslims], it can be divided into five shares if the Government so decides. In this case, the four shares will be distributed [in accordance with the details laid down by the Law]. But if the government decides to leave it [in the hands of the original occupants], it may do so, just as 'Umar had done in the case of the land of Sawad. The occupants would pay the *Kharaj* and the one-fifth [of its total income] would be distributed in accordance with the rules laid down in the Book of Allah.

37. It has come down to us about Abu Bakr, 'Umar, 'Uthman and Ali (may Allah be pleased with them) that they used to distribute one-fifth among the three categories of those entitled to the shares: the orphans, the destitute and the wayfarers.

38. While distributing the spoils, two shares will be allocated to the rider and one share to the foot-soldier. According to Abū Ḥanīfah, a beast will not be given preference to the foot-soldier: this has come down to us from 'Umar ibn al-Khattab. But according to Abu Yusuf and Muhammad ibn al-Hasan al-Shaybānī), a rider will be given three shares: two shares for his horse and one share for himself, while there will be one share for the foot-soldier. In this context, the rider of a mule and the foot-soldier will be equal, and the rider of a horse of a low breed [*birdhawn*] and that of a high breed will also be equal.

39. When a warrior enters the Territory of War along with the army as a rider but his horse perishes or gets wounded before he secures the spoils, he will have the share of a rider. But if he enters as a foot-soldier and then buys a horse and fights on it, he will have the share of a foot-soldier. A rider who enters the Territory of War along with his horse will have the share of a rider whether he fights on the horse, on foot, in a boat, or in a vessel, etc.

40. If a warrior dies before the booty is taken to the Territory of Islam, there will be no share for him in it. If he dies after it was taken to the Territory of Islam, then his share will be handed down as his inheritance. When an army gets hold of a booty, but before it carries it to the Territory of Islam, another army joins them as their reinforcement, and none of the two faces the enemy till the spoils

are carried to the Territory of Islam, all of them will be co-sharers in the spoils.

41. If a slave accompanies his master and fights, he should be given a gift [rather than the regular share in the spoils of war]. Likewise, a child, a woman, a *Dhimmi* and a *Mukatab* should be given gifts. But if a slave merely serves his master [but does not fight], he will not be given any gift. Also, if the traders associated with the army do not fight [they will not be given any gifts]. According to Abū Ḥanīfah and Muhammad [ibn al-Hasan al-Shaybānī], only one horse will receive his share, but Abu Yusuf says that two horses will get their shares but not more than two.

42. If somebody is wounded in the war or made captive, and in the meantime, the [Muslim] army gets some booty before the wounds of the injured person have healed or the captive returns [without participating in the war] along with them before the booty is brought [to the Territory of Islam], both of them will be considered to be entitled to shares in the booty. If someone from the people of the Territory of War embraces Islam and joins them [i.e.,,, the Muslim army] or a Muslim trader or a repenting apostate joins the [Muslim] army, these persons will not be included among the recipients of the booty except when they face an opportunity to fight, and they do actually fight along with the army.

43. It is not advisable for the *Imam* [the Government] to donate something by way of *Nafl* (or supererogatory share) to someone out of the booty that he had himself acquired. Such supererogatory share can only be announced before the acquisition of the booty by such words: "Whosoever kills a person [from the enemy] will have his belongings": Or "Whosoever acquires something will have it".

Such announcements were likely to have been made to encourage people to fight. If someone takes fodder out of the booty and after returning to the Territory of Islam something is surplus out of that [fodder], it should be returned to the booty in case it has not yet been distributed. In case it has already been distributed, it should be sold, and its price should be given away as charity. If someone from the army had given it as a loan to somebody, it would not be advisable for the latter to take anything out of it.

44. If someone from the army manumits a slave girl from the booty, such manumission will not be held valid under *Istiḥsan* [juristic preference]. If he sought to impregnate her and she bore a child from him, it would not be lawful; the parentage of the child would not be established, and the person would be required to pay the damages. The slave girl and the child will be returned to the booty. If someone steals something from the booty, his hand will not be cut, and so will his servant and all his relatives in the prohibited degree. If, at the time of the distribution of the booty, a slave-girl falls in the common share of a group of battalions, and a person from among them manumits her, it will be valid if they are one hundred or less. I do not prescribe any time limit for this.

45. When the army takes a woman captive, followed by her husband, who is also taken captive sooner or later, and either the woman does not have menses during that period or has had up to three menses, but she is not taken out of the Territory of War before her husband is taken, their marriage shall continue. Whosoever of the two is taken captive and brought to the Territory of Islam before the other, their marriage shall cease to exist.

Chapter III : Acquisition of Muslim property earlier taken away by non-Muslims as Booty

46. If a Muslim finds in the booty something from his own property which had been earlier acquired and taken possession of by the Polytheists [i.e., non-Muslims], he will be entitled to it without any consideration before the distribution of the booty, provided he produces a proof thereof. But if he finds it after the distribution [of the booty], he can take it on payment of its price. As regards dirham, *dinār* [i.e.,, cash] and commodities that are weighed and measured, no one has any access to them because in case someone acquires them, he may acquire them only in lieu of a similar commodity. If someone finds a slave of his who had earlier fled away to them and now he has fallen in the share of someone from the [Muslim] army, he [the original owner] can take him back without any consideration. However, he [in whose share the slave has now fallen] will be paid his price from the exchequer. If he finds him [i.e., the runaway slave] in possession of someone who had purchased him from some men of the Territory of War, he can take him back without paying any price, according to *Imam* Abū Ḥanīfah. According to Abu Yusuf and Muhammad [ibn al-Hasan al-Shaybānī], he can take him back after paying the price in case the infidels had overpowered him in their own territory, but if they had taken him captive when he came to them himself, his master can take him back from his purchaser after paying the price.

47. In case the people of the Territory of War presented him as a gift to someone, his [original] master could take him back after paying the price. Likewise, if the purchaser sold him to some other person,

the master can take him back from the second purchaser by paying the same price on which the latter had purchased him. The purchaser's statement about the price will be acceptable on oath [in case of a dispute between the parties about the amount of price]. In case someone purchased him from the people of the Territory of War but he was taken captive again before his [original] master could claim him, in the meantime, another person purchased him, and after his original master made his claim, the latter will have no claim over him and the first purchaser will be entitled to get him back on paying the price. In case he [i.e.,, the first purchaser] takes him, the original master will have a right to take him by paying the two prices.

48. When the enemy makes a slave captive while he is answerable for a crime of murder, intentional or accidental, or for a debt, he will continue to be answerable as before if he comes back to his master on the basis of the latter's first title of ownership whatever be the mode of his coming back. But if the slave does not come back to him [i.e.,, to his original master] or comes to him on the basis of some fresh ownership, he will be absolved of the liability of accidental homicide. As to the liability in the case of intentional murder or debt, it will continue as before and he will be answerable in both cases.

49. If a captive slave falls in the lot of a person who manumits him or declares his manumission at his death" before the original master turns up, he can do so and the original master shall have no claim upon him. If she is a slave girl and he [i.e.,, the person in whose lot she has fallen] gives her in marriage to someone and she gives birth to the child of her husband, the original master will have a right to own her as well her child, but he will have no right to cancel the

marriage. If the person [in whose share she has fallen] has received her *urq* or the *arsh* of an offence committed against her, the original master will have no claim to it [i.e., *urq* or *arsh*]. In case she has not been given in marriage to anyone, he may have sexual relations with her even if he knew her background.

50. If the person made captive belongs to a child orphan, his guardian may take him from his purchaser by paying the price. But the guardian cannot take him for himself. If a slave-girl has been mortgaged for one thousand *dirhams*, which is also her price, and the enemy makes her captive, after which someone purchases her for one thousand *dirhams,* the mortgagee will have superior rights to her. If he [the mortgagee] refuses to take her, her master will have a superior right to take her by paying the price. If he [the master] takes her, she will be no more a mortgage because he has already redeemed her for one thousand *dirhams*. This will be like a wrong committed by her as if the mortgagee had refused to redeem her and the mortgager had redeemed her. But if the price is less than one thousand *dirhams*, the mortgagee will have the right to pay the price which the master had paid for her. She will be considered as mortgaged with him as before if he so likes; otherwise, he may leave her. This issue has been explained in *al-Jami' al-Kabir.* If she was given into his possession by way of trust, lending or hiring, he will have no right to take her back; rather, the right to own her shall remain with her master. If she has had a husband before being held captive, their marriage will continue.

51. If the enemy gains control over the property of the Muslims, takes it into his possession and acquires it, and a Muslim trader, who happens to be there in their territory on the permission of security, he may lawfully purchase that property from them. If the property

so purchased includes a slave-girl, he may have sexual relations with her. If a person made captive [by the enemy] is a slave of a Muslim and is sold by their [i.e.,, enemies] government to someone from the Territory of War and the purchaser manumits him he may lawfully do it and his manumission will be valid.

52. If the people of the Territory of War who had acquired a property of the Muslims embraced Islam and agreed to become *Guaranteed Citizens*, the property would remain theirs, and the Muslims would have no title over that property. Likewise, if a *Harb* comes to the Territory of Islam on permission of security along with something out of that property in order to sell it, its previous Muslim owner shall have no claim to that property.

53. If a child is made captive from the Territory of War and is brought to the Territory of Islam without his parents and dies before reaching the age of understanding, his funeral prayer will be offered. If one of his parents is also [made captive and] brought along with him, or the child. is brought from one side and one of the parents from another side at the same time, or one of his parents is brought before him, his funeral prayer will not be offered." But if the child is brought first [and then dies], his funeral prayer will be offered. As long as the captives are disbelievers and do not enter the fold of Islam, there is no harm if they are sold to the People of the *Dhimmah* (*Guaranteed Citizens*); but they shall not be sold to the people of the Territory of War."

54. The *Imam* [i.e.,, the Islamic government] may execute the males [from amongst the prisoners]; or he may not execute them and distribute them among the army, taking into consideration which is best for the Muslims. But if they embrace Islam, he shall not execute

them; rather, he may distribute them. If they claim that they were given *aman* [security] and a group of Muslims confirms that they have pledged them security, their statement will not be accepted as true. If a group of just [*udul* Muslims give testimony against another group of Muslims that these [latter] have pledged them security while they were fully protected, their testimony will be valid.

55. Blind, crippled and lunatic prisoners will not be executed. Water may be released to the dwellings of the people at war [against the Muslims]; their city may be put to fire [to force them to surrender], and mangonel may be used against them, even though they have among them Muslim children or other persons, prisoners or traders. So also, if they take shelter behind them. However, a Muslim should aim his fire at the enemy. But if a Muslim from amongst them [i.e.,, the enemy] is hit by it, there is neither any *kaffarah* [expiation] nor any *Diyah* is to be paid.

56. When a Muslim enters the Territory of War with permission of security, and he has a slave girl of his own in their possession, I would not like him to take possession of her by force or other illegal means or to have sexual relations with her. But if she a *mudabbar* or *umm walad,* I would not disapprove of it. If someone is a prisoner with them, I would not disapprove of his taking possession of his slave girl by force or any other means or even stealing her. I would not disapprove that he kills from amongst them whom he can and take from their property whatever he can.

57. If a *Ḥarbi* embraces Islam while he is still in the Territory of War and then the Muslims conquer that territory, his property, slaves and the minor children in his possession will be left to him. But his landed property and his house will be considered to be a *fay*, as well

as his adult children, his pregnant wife, and her embryo. If he had come to the Territory of Islam and embraced Islam there, after which his territory was conquered [by the Muslims], his family and property would be considered to be *fay*. If he had embraced Islam in the Territory of War and then entered the Territory of Islam, after which the Muslims conquer his territory, all his property there will be *fay*, except his minor children. Whatever he has by way of deposit, either with a Muslim or a *Dhimmi* will also be considered to be *fay*.

58. When a Muslim or a *Dhimmi* enters the Territory of War with the permission of security (*aman*) as a trader and acquires there some property, movable or immovable, all this property will remain in his ownership in case the Muslims conquer that property, except houses and other landed property which will be considered to be *fay*. Those of his adult slaves who have taken part in the battle will also be considered *fay*. Likewise, if he has a *Harbi* wife who is pregnant from him shall be considered *fay* along with her embryo. Whatever deposits he has with a *Harbi* or a *Dhimmi* will continue to be his property and will not be considered to be *fay*. So also, if he had already moved to the Territory of Islam. If the Muslims [after conquering the Territory of War] get hold of that deposit and distribute it among themselves by way of booty, its original owner, as and when he comes, will take it without paying the price because this is the property of a Muslim which had not been acquired by the disbelievers. If the disbelievers kill this Muslim in their territory and take his property, and then the Muslims conquer them, that property will be returned to the heirs of the person killed. If they have already distributed it and then the heirs come, they can take the property after paying the price; however, they will not be entitled to take the gold and silver (i.e.,, cash). If these disbelievers

[who own that property] enter the fold of Islam or enter into a treaty of peace, they will not be accountable for anything either of the property or blood of the person killed.

59. A Muslim enters the Territory of War with the permission of security (*aman*) and buys a slave child, male or female, and leaves them behind after manumitting them; they grow up as disbelievers; now, if the Muslims conquer their territory, they will be considered *Fay* and his manumission will not be treated as a ground for their freedom because his manumission in that territory is void.

60. When a Muslim goes to the Territory of War as a trader, or a prisoner, or someone embraces Islam there and grants security to the people of the Territory of War [on behalf of the Muslims], the security given to them shall be void. But if someone from amongst the [Muslim] army, male or female, grants security to a group of the *People of war*, the security shall be valid. If the security is given by a [Muslim] slave, his security will be valid if he is among those fighting along with their masters; but if he is not one of those who fought, the security granted by him will not be valid. But Muhammad (i.e., Shaybānī) says that his security shall be valid in both cases.

61. The security given by a *Dhimmi* who is there only to assist the Muslims is void.

62. If the *Imam* [i.e.,, the Government] declares: "Whosoever gets something it will be his", and a man gets a slave girl and fulfils the requirements of *istibra,*" Muhammad [ibn al-Hasan al-Shaybānī] says that he should neither have sexual relations with her nor sell her before taking her to the Territory of Islam.

63. When a group [of Muslim soldiers] from a contingent or an army go out and acquire some booty, he [Muhammad ibn al-Hassan al-Shaybānī] says one-fifth of it should be recovered [for the state], and the rest should be distributed among them as well as among the rest of the army. It is immaterial whether they had gone with the permission of the *Imam* (Supreme Commander) or not. Such will be the case if only one individual does that because the battalion and the army are, in fact, a source of support and help for them. The same is the case with a person whom the leader had sent for patrolling, and he got some booty. In case they had gone out from a big city like Missisah or Malaṭiyah and their leader had sent them along with an expedition, and they got some booty, the people of the city shall have no share from that booty.

64. If one or two persons go from such big cities with the permission of the *Imam* (Supreme Commander) and get some booty, in this case, one-fifth will not be recovered; the entire booty will go to those who get it. But if the booty includes a slave girl, there should be no sexual relations with her before her being taken [to the Territory of Islam].

65. If a Muslim enters their territory with the permission of security and buys a slave girl who is a Scriptuary, he can have sexual relations with her while still in that territory, provided the requirements of *istibra* are met. I [i.e., Shaybānī] do not like a Muslim to have sexual relations with his wife or slave-girl while in the Territory of War lest issues are born to him there [who may in some eventuality be exposed to slavery, a situation which is the duty of the Islamic State to avoid].

66. If the Governor of Syria, [for example], goes out to fight along with a big army and lays siege to a city for a long period of time, he

should neither offer full prayers nor organize the Friday prayers even though he might be implementing the Hudud [the prescribed punishments] because he enjoys the concessions allowed to a traveller.

67. When a group of Muslims intends to fight against a Territory of War, and they do not possess force or wealth, they may provide equipment to one another. Those who do not go out may help those who do. But if they have sufficient force or the government has sufficient wealth, I would not approve of it [i.e., soldiers helping themselves].

68. If a person finds someone else to look after the ward and watch effectively, I prefer for him to be busy with prayers. But if he does not find anybody to effectively look after it, I would prefer for him to be busy in guarding [the frontier].

69. If a Muslim is stabbed with a lance in his belly, I do not disapprove of his walking to his enemy while the lance is still in his belly in order to strike him with a sword. I will not consider him to be assisting his enemy in taking his own life. When the Muslims are aboard a ship and fire is thrown at them in the ship itself, they may either remain [aboard the ship] in spite of the fire or throw themselves into the sea.

Chapter IV: Management of *Kharaj*

70. When the *Imam* [Government] declares a group of infidels to be the *Guaranteed Citizens*, he shall impose the *Kharaj* per capita as well as on the lands according to their capacity. It has been reported to us that 'Umar had imposed a per capita levy on all cultivable lands: one dirham and one qafiz on one *jarib* of land, on one *jarib* of grapes ten *dirhams*; five *dirhams* on one *jarib* of ripe dates; twelve *dirhams*, twenty-four *dirhams* and forth-eight *dirhams* in three categories on men: the *Kharaj* levied on the poor who had no wealth but still could pay was twelve *dirhams*; the poor who had some wealth had to pay twenty-four *dirhams*, and the rich had to pay forty-eight *dirhams*.

71. Nothing will be levied on women and children; nor anything on the blind, the old, the lunatic, the disabled, and the poor who are unable to work.

72. No *Kharaj* will be levied on the slaves. There is no levy on the property of the *Guaranteed Citizens* in their respective homelands. The levy on the lands of their children, women and *Mukatabs* is the same as on their men.

73. Whoever enters the fold of Islam from amongst the *Guaranteed Citizens* before the completion of the year or after its completion but before the recovery of the *Kharaj* levied on him, his *Kharaj* will be dropped. Likewise, is the case if he dies as an infidel. If he does not die and several years pass without any recovery being made from him, nothing will be recovered from him except the *Kharaj* of that particular year, according to *Imam* Abū Ḥanīfah. But according to Abu Yusuf and Muhammad [ibn al-Hasan al-Shybani], all previous dues will be recovered from him.

74. The *Kharaj* levied on the land will be recovered only once in a year, even though its owner grows several crops on it. But if he leaves the land uncultivated, *Kharaj* will not be dropped. If he cultivates the land but the produce is destroyed due to some natural calamity, the owner will not be required to pay the *Kharaj.*

75. If a *Guaranteed Citizen* embraces Islam while in possession of a land he will be required to pay its *Kharaj* as before. It is not disapproved (*makruh*) if a Muslim pays the *Kharaj* levied on land or if he purchases land from the *Guaranteed Citizens.*

76. If a Taghlibite purchases the Kharāji land, he will have to pay the *Kharaj* as was paid before. If he purchases an *'Ushr* land he will be required to pay double the *'Ushr*. Likewise, their women and children [will pay double the *'Ushr*].

77. According to Muhammad [ibn al-Hasan al-Shaybānī], when a land is a land of *'Ushr,* it will remain a land of *'Ushr* for good: its status will not be changed by the change of ownership as a result of a sale. Also, the land of *Kharaj* will remain the land of *Kharaj* for good: its status will not be changed by the change of ownership as a result of the sale. Don't you see that its status would not change if it was purchased by a *Mukatab* or by a minor? You may see that if a Dhimmi or a Taghlibite purchases the land of Makkah in the territory of Haram, it will not change its status as a *Ushri* land of Makkah.

78. If a *Harbi* enters the Territory of Islam after seeking due security and marries a woman there, he will not, ipso facto, become a *Dhimmi* except when he settles down there permanently, and *Kharaj* is imposed on him. If he purchases a Kharāji land and cultivates it he will be liable to pay the per capita *Kharaj* as well as the *Kharaj* of land. On the other hand, if a *Harbi* woman entering [the Territory of Islam]

with security marries a Muslim or a *Dhimmi,* she will be considered to have settled down and shall, [*ipso facto*], become a *Dhimmi.*

Chapter V: Peace, Reconciliation and Armistice among Rulers

79. If a ruler from amongst the rulers of the Territory of War having a vast land inhabited by a people of his kingdom who are considered to be his slaves and he sells whomever he likes from among them, enters into an agreement of peace with the Muslims and becomes a *Guaranteed Citizen* of the Islamic state, his people will be considered to be his slaves as they used to be before. He will have the right to sell them if he likes. If an enemy, other than the Muslims with whom they had entered into an agreement of peace, conquers them and they are rescued by these Muslims from the hands of the enemy, they will, said [Shaybānī], be returned to that ruler without any consideration before they are distributed and with consideration after they are distributed. Likewise, if the ruler and his people embrace Islam or his people embrace Islam without him, they will remain his slaves as they were before.

80. If a ruler demands at the time of entering into an agreement of guarantee that he should be left free to rule his people and run his government as he likes by killing people, hanging them and doing with them other acts that are not permissible in Islam, this demand will not be acceded to. If the agreement of truce or guarantee is entered into on the basis of such conditions, it will be void to the extent of what is unlawful in Islam. If he [i.e.,, the ruler] agrees to this provision, it is well and good; otherwise, he and his colleagues should be provided safe return to their place of security. If, after entering into an agreement of guarantee, it transpires that he [the ruler] informs the infidels about the weak points and secrets of the

Muslims and harbours the spies of the enemy, this act will not be considered to be a violation of the agreement but he may be punished for this act and may be imprisoned. Likewise, if he still commits murder of Muslims or his people do it, this also will not be considered to be a violation of the agreement on his part. However, the person against whom the commission of this act is established on the basis of proof will be liable to the punishment of *qisas.*

81. If the murderer is not known and the victim is found in one of their [i.e. non-Muslims'] villages, he should take fifty oaths to the effect that he neither killed the victim nor knew the murderer who had killed him. After taking oath, he will be required to pay *Diyah.* The residents of the village will not be required to take oath along with him because they are his slaves [and not free men]. But if they are freemen, they will be liable to *qasamah* as well as *Diyah.*

82. If a people of the Territory of War request for an agreement of peace for an indefinite number of years without anything [i.e.,, without the payment of any tribute], the *Imam* should look into this request: if he finds it good for the Muslims due to their strong position or due to some other consideration, he may accede to this request. If, after making the agreement of peace, he looks into it and finds it harmful for the Muslims, he should publicly renounce the agreement and resume war.

Section: Agreement of peace on the condition that Muslims should pay a particular amount annually to the disbelievers.

83. When the enemy besieges the Muslims in a city and asks the Muslims to enter into an agreement of peace on the condition that the Muslims should pay a particular amount annually to them and the Muslims face a threat to their existence and feel that this agreement of peace is good for them, Shaybānī says that there is no harm if they enter into it.

84. If a Muslim people of the Territory of War offer to enter into an agreement of peace [with the Muslim state] for a particular number of years on the condition that the people of the Territory of War would pay a specific amount of money by way of *Kharaj* annually to the Muslims provided that they should not be asked to submit themselves to the laws of Islam in their own country, this offer will not be accepted save when it is good for the Muslims. If it is good for the Muslims and the terms of the agreement include that they will pay the Muslims one hundred slaves, it will not be allowed if they bring these one hundred persons as slaves from amongst themselves because the agreement of peace has guaranteed [the protection of] their group as well as their children. Suppose the agreement of peace has taken place on the condition that they will give one hundred particular slaves in the beginning of every year, stipulating that: "these particular slaves will be yours in consideration of the security given to us, and we enter into the agreement of peace with you for a future period of three years on the condition that we will give you any one hundred slaves from amongst our slaves", says Shaybānī, "it is allowed". If this agreement takes place and then a Muslim steals something from them [while still in the battlefield], no one has the right even to purchase it from him.

85. If a group of the people of the Territory of War attack them, it is allowed to purchase from them what they have captured of their

property and the slaves. Traders will not be prevented from carrying on their trade with them except in the horses, the weaponry, the steel crafts and the like. Because they are not *Guaranteed Citizens*; they have only entered into [a temporary] agreement of peace. If any of them enters the Territory of Islam without acquiring a fresh permission of security apart from his peace agreement, he will not be disturbed.

86. When a *Musta'min* [i.e., a citizen of the Territory of War entering the Territory of Islam with the permission of security] purchases a Muslim or a *Dhimmi* slave in the Territory of Islam, or one of his slaves who has come along with him embraces Islam, he will not be allowed to take him [i.e.,, the Muslim or *Dhimmi* slave] back to the Territory of War. When a *Musta'min* return to the Territory of War after incurring debts in the Territory of Islam, depositing some money with someone or granting *tadbir* to a slave, after which he is made captive [in a subsequent battle], his territory is subjugated, and he is eventually killed, all his debts and deposits will become null and void. Likewise, his slaves will also cease to be his slaves [as they will go to the Muslim state], except those who had been granted *tadbir* in the Territory of Islam. These latter will be considered to be free.

Section: Acceptance of the evidence of the People of the Guarantee in favour of the heirs of a *Musta'min* who dies in our territory while the Heirs are still in the Territory of War.

87. When a *Musta'min* dies in the Territory of Islam, leaving behind some property while his heirs are still in the Territory of War, Shaybānī says that his property will be retained until his heirs come and produce evidence thereto. If they produce witnesses from amongst the People of the Guarantee, their evidence will be accepted by way of juristic preference. In this respect, any letter written by their government will not be accepted even if a group of Muslims testify in its favour and put their seal on it.

88. When a citizen of the Territory of War who has entered the Territory of Islam with a bond of security wants to go back to the Territory of War, he will not be allowed to take with him any beast of burden, weaponry, steel or iron items or the slaves, Muslims or non- Muslims, purchased from the Territory of Islam. However, he will not be prevented from taking back with him what he had himself brought [from the Territory of War]. If he had brought a sword with him and has now purchased a bow or a lance in its place, he will not be permitted to take it back in lieu of his sword; likewise, if he replaces his sword with a better one [he will not be allowed to take the new one with him]. However, if the new one is just like the former or inferior to it, he will not be prevented from taking it back. He will be allowed to take whatever belongings he may like with him. If a citizen of the Territory of War sends his slave as a trader to the Territory of Islam with the permission of security and the slave embraces Islam while in the Territory of Islam, he will be sold here and the price will be sent to its owner in the Territory of War.

Section: A *Harbi* found in the Territory of Islam claiming to be an envoy.

89. If a *Harbi* is found in the Territory of Islam and claims to be an emissary and produces a letter from his King to this effect, he will be provided security if the letter is confirmed to be really from the King. He will be secure till he delivers the message and returns [to his territory]. But if the letter is not confirmed to be from the King, the man and his belongings shall be considered to be *fay*. Likewise, if he claims to have entered with the permission of security [without any proof], his claim will not be accepted, and he will be taken as *fay*.

90. When a group of *Harbis* [i.e., the *People of war*] come over [to the Territory of Islam] with permission of security, no intervention will be made in whatever mutual debts and transactions have taken place among them in the Territory of War. But if these transactions take place in the Territory of Islam, they shall be liable therefor.

91. If a *Harbi* enters the Territory of Islam without a permission of security, he will be considered to be the slave of anyone who takes him captive. If he embraces Islam before being made captive by anyone, he is free according to Abu Yusuf and Muhammad [ibn al-Hasan al- Shaybānī]. But according to Abū Ḥanīfah, he will be considered *fay* for the collectivity of the Muslims, whether taken captive before accepting Islam or after it. If he enters the *Harams* before being taken captive, he will not be arrested; however, he will not be provided food, drink or shelter so that he comes out. Anybody who arrests him in the Haram will be a wrong-doer. The injunction in this matter is in accordance with the discussion made in the context of *Hill*.

92. When a Muslim enters the Territory of War with permission of security and enters with them into transactions of debts and loans or they misappropriate each other's property no decree shall be issued inter se in respect of these matters [by a Muslim court]. There will be no harm if he enters with them into a contract of sale of two *dirhams* for one either on cash or on credit or enters with them into a dealing involving liquor or of swine [i.e. pork]. Because, according to Abū Ḥanīfah and Muhammad [ibn al-Hasan al-Shaybānī], it is lawful for him to take their money with their permission. But Abu Yusuf says none of these transactions is allowed to him.

93. When a *Harbi* comes over to us with permission of security, it will not be lawful for a Muslim to enter with him into any transaction of this kind. If a Muslim kills him intentionally or mistakenly, he will not be liable to *Qisas*; however, he will have to pay the *Diyah* of a Muslim freeman.

Chapter VI: Inter-marriages of the people of war and the entry of the traders in their territory with a permission of security

94. If a *Harbi* man marries a *Harbi* woman already having a husband, and then both of them [i.e., the woman and her new husband] embrace Islam and come over to us, she will not be considered to be his lawful wife unless a fresh marriage is solemnized between them. If a *Harbi* marries four women and then all of them are taken as prisoners of war [and declared slaves by the Muslim state] their previous marriages will not be recognized to be subsisting.

95. The animals slaughtered by the People of the Book from amongst them [i.e. from amongst the *Harbis*] are lawful.

Section: When the people of this territory acquire captives from amongst the other *Harbis*.

96. If a Muslim entering the Territory of War with their permission kills one of their men or consumes his property, he will not be liable for any compensation after their return. So will be the case also if they [i.e., the *Harbis*] kill him. I would not like a Muslim entering their territory with permission to commit any kind of treachery not allowed under his *Din*. If he commits any treachery to them, takes their property and brings it to the Territory of Islam, I would not like the Muslims to buy it if they know it. However, if anybody buys it, I will accept [this purchase] as valid. If she is a slave-girl, I would not like him to take her as a concubine. But if the people of this territory

[i.e. *Harbis*] acquire captives from some other Territory of War, a Muslim may purchase from them. Also, if the people of the territory in which the Muslim happens to be take some prisoners as captives, I think that the Muslims may buy [a slave] from them.

97. Likewise, if the Muslims enter into an agreement of friendship (*muwada'ah*) with a *People of war* and later on they are attacked by another *People of war* who declare the former to have become slaves. a Muslim can purchase a slave from the latter. But if some Muslims make them captives, committing treachery with the people of this treaty of friendship, it will not be allowed for the Muslims to purchase any of these slaves. In case anyone purchases one, I will order him to revoke the deal.

98. If a group of Muslims happen to be in the Territory of War with permission of security and the territory is attacked by another *People of war* it will not be permissible for these Muslims to fight along with them because the laws of polytheism are supreme. However, if the Muslims feel threatened by them, they may fight in their own defence.

99. If the people of the Territory of War attack the territory of the Muslims, make the free Muslim women and children, captives and along with them pass by the Muslims residing there [temporarily] under permission of security, they have no option except to revoke the covenant and fight for Muslim women and children if they have the capability to fight. Likewise, if they [i.e. *People of war*] attack a group of non-Muslim citizens of the Islamic state who pay *Kharaj* and make their women and children captives. Likewise, if there are some Muslims in the area of the Khawarij whom the *Harbis* have attacked,

these Muslims will have no option except to fight along with the Khawarij to defend the honor and homeland of the Muslims.

Chapter VII : Injunctions about the Apostates

100. If a Muslim reverts from Islam, he will be invited to understand Islam. If he accepts Islam, it is well and good; otherwise, he will be executed immediately. However, if he demands that he must be given some time [to further think over it] he should be given a period of three days period [to think further].

101. Similar reports have come down to us from the Holy Prophet (peace be on him) about the execution of the apostate.

102. Similar reports have come down to us from 'Ali, may Allah be pleased with him, Ibn Mas'ud and Mu'adh. If the apostate refuses to re- embrace Islam he should be executed. His inheritance shall be distributed among his Muslim heirs according to the shares laid down by Allah.

103. It has been transmitted to us that 'Ali ibn Abi Talib, may Allah be pleased with him, executed an apostate and distributed his property among his Muslim heirs according to the shares laid down by Allah, the Exalted.

104. Likewise, if the apostate moves away to the Territory of War, the *Imam* shall distribute his inheritance among his heirs. His moving away to that territory will be treated as his death. The debts incurred by him shall, however, be paid off; his female-slaves who have already given birth to his children shall stand manumitted; so also, his *Mudabbar*- slaves; the debts he owed [to others] shall also become due; his wills shall become null and void; his [divorced] wife shall also inherit from him if she is still in her waiting period (*'iddah*).

105. None of these actions shall be taken as long as the apostate is still a resident of the Territory of Islam. If the *Imam* has taken all these steps after his moving away to the Territory of War but he comes back after repenting his action, the steps taken by the *Imam* shall stand enforced. However, if he [i.e. the repenting apostate] finds some of his property intact in the possession of his heir he can take it back from him. But if none of these steps were taken by the *Imam* before he came back after repenting, all his property will be given back to him.

106. All the actions taken by an apostate during the period of his apostasy, such as sale, purchase, manumission, *tadbir*, *kitabah*, gift, consummation of concubinage, claim of parentage, will be valid if he re-enters the fold of Islam and void if he moves away to the Territory of War. In the latter case, the state shall distribute his property [among his legal heirs], except for the parentage which will be established [on the basis of his claim], and the child will inherit along with other heirs.

107. When an apostate manumits his slave and, at the same time or soon after that, his son also manumits him, and he does not have any other heir, the manumission of both will be invalid. If the son dies leaving behind a manumitter and the father is still apostate and, then the father also dies leaving behind a manumitter of his own, the inheritance of the father will go to his manumitter rather than the manumitter of the son.

108. The property earned by the apostate during the period of his apostasy shall be considered *fay*, according to Abū Ḥanīfah. But Abu Yusuf and Muḥammad [ibn al-Hasan al-Shaybānī] say that his earnings will go to his heirs, and nothing out of his earnings in the

Territory of Islam can be treated as *fay*. His sale, purchase and manumission during his apostasy are valid. However, Muhammad [ibn al-Hasan al-Shaybānī] says he will be treated like a sick man.

109. An animal slaughtered by an apostate cannot be eaten even though he becomes a Christian.

110. If an apostate commits a criminal offence [against the person of somebody], his Aqilah will not be required to pay any blood money, and all these payments will be made from his own property. Likewise, whatever has been usurped or illegally possessed by an apostate or destroyed by him of other's property [will be compensated from his own pocket]. If he has no property except that which he has earned during his apostasy, it will be paid out of it. Any offence against the person of the apostate will be treated as unprotected by law.

111. If a Muslim cuts, the hand of another Muslim, intentionally or unintentionally, after which the victim renounces Islam and moves away to the Territory of War and dies there, or dies before moving away to the Territory of War, or dies thereafter re-embracing Islam, in all these cases the offender [i.e. the one who cut the hand] will pay the blood- money from his own pocket if the offence was intentional. It will be paid by his *'Aqilah* if it was unintentional, except in one situation. When the victim embraces Islam before moving away to the Territory of War and dies, in this case, the offender will pay the *Diyah* of life [i.e., full *Diyah*], according to Abū Ḥanīfah and Abu Yusuf; while Muhammad [ibn al-Hasan al-Shaybānī] says that he will pay only the *Diyah* [i.e.,, the arsh] of hand. If the apostate had himself cut the hand of somebody, then he [i.e.,, the apostate] himself was executed and, in the meanwhile, the

victim [whose hand was cut), a Muslim, dies as a result of this injury, the offender will not be liable to anything if the offence was intentional while his Aqilah will be liable to pay the *Diyah* if it was unintentional. If the offence had taken place while the offender was an apostate, the *Diyah* in respect of an unintentional homicide will be paid from the offender's property; in case he does not have any property except that which he has earned during his apostasy, I [i.e., Shaybānī] will take it from such property [to satisfy the requirement of the *Diyah*].

112. A female apostate will not be executed. Rather, she will be imprisoned for life or until she re-embraces Islam. It has come down to us from Ibn 'Abbas that he said: "When a woman apostatizes from Islam, she will be imprisoned and not executed". It has also come down to us from the Messenger of Allah, peace be on him, that he had prohibited the killing of the women of the polytheists on the battlefield. I would prefer to spare her from killing in this case also. Her property and personal belongings will be hers. Her actions in the contracts of sale, purchase, manumission and gift shall all be valid.

113. In case she dies in prison or moves away to the Territory of War, her property will be distributed among her heirs according to the shares laid down by the Almighty Allah, as we have already explained in the case of a male apostate. Her husband will inherit nothing from her except in case she apostatizes while she is in her last illness [i.e.,, death bed] and dies before the completion of her waiting period [*'Iddah*], in which case he will inherit from her. If she moves away to the Territory of War, her husband can marry her sister even before the completion of her waiting period. 136 If she is made captive and returns as a Muslim, this will not affect the

marriage of her [former] husband. In case of captivity, she will be regarded as *Fay* and shall be forced to accept Islam. If she returns as a Muslim, she may remarry at the very moment. If she gives birth to a child in the Territory of War and is made captive along with the child, the child will also be considered as *Fay* along with the mother. Abu Yusuf used to say: "A female apostate will be executed like a very old man [or shaykh fani] who is executed on account of apostasy if he does not repent". He [Abu Yusuf] used to prohibit the killing of persons [from amongst the personnel of the enemy] even inside the Territory of War, who are very advanced in age; but later on, he returned to the view of Abū Ḥanīfah.

114. When a female apostate is brought to the *Imam* [on the charge of apostasy] but she says she never apostatized and is prepared to testify that "There is none to be worshipped except Allah and that Muhammad is the Messenger of Allah, it will be considered to be repentance on her part.

115. A male slave will be liable to execution on conviction of apostasy. His personal belongings will go to his master. A female slave will not be executed but will be imprisoned. In case her masters need her services, she will be handed over to them, and they will be required to secure her re-entry in Islam.

116. Offences committed by slaves, male, female or *Mukatab*, during their apostasy, shall be treated like their offence without apostasy. Offences committed against them during their apostasy shall be regarded as non-existent. There shall be no liability on the killer of a female apostate, whether she is a free woman or a slave, because according to some jurists, she is already liable to execution.

117. When a person sells his apostate slave or his apostate female slave, the sale will be valid, and the apostasy shall be recognized as a defect in respect of both of them.

118. If a *Mudabbar* slave-girl or an Umm Walad apostatizes and moves away to the Territory of War and, in the meantime, her master dies in the Territory of Islam, and she is brought back as a captive [to the Territory of Islam], Shaybānī says, she will be regarded as *fay*. If a slave and his master apostatize and move away to the Territory of War, the master dies while still there, and the slave is brought as a captive; Shaybānī says he will be regarded as *fay* and will be executed if he does not re-embrace Islam. Likewise, whatever property an apostate takes away with him will [on recovery] be regarded as *fay*. In case he comes to the Territory of Islam as an aggressor [for loot and plunder] and takes away some of the property which had been distributed among his heirs and is killed afterwards as an apostate or that property is retrieved, in both the cases the property will be given back to his heirs without any price, if not yet distributed [among the warriors] and with price if already distributed. Likewise, if a slave apostatizes and runs away with the property of his master to the Territory of War and is taken back as a captive, he will not be regarded as *Fay* but will be returned to his master.

119. When a group of people renounce Islam, fight against the Muslims, and obtain control over a city out of their cities in an area surrounded by the Territory of War, and they also have their women and children along with them who are also apostates with no Muslims inside the city and only the apostates fighting against them [i.e., the Muslim army] and the Muslim army subjugates them, he [Shaybānī] says that in this case all men shall be executed and

anybody who re-embraces Islam shall be set free; the women, children and the property shall be considered as *Fay* out of which one-fifth will be rendered [to the public exchequer]. If any woman out of these apostates falls into the lot of somebody, it will not be lawful for him to have sexual relations with her as long as she remains apostate, even though she is a Jew or a Christian. If she had some debt to pay while she was a Muslim, that debt would become null and void in her captivity.

120. When the people of a city from amongst the Muslims become apostates and get control over that city while there is still a group of Muslims living peacefully but whose wives have also become apostates along with the group of men, after which the Muslims get back the control of the city and subjugate them, they [i.e. apostates] will all be considered as freemen, but they will be forced to re-enter Islam. Abul- Fadl [the commentator] says: "By this, he [i.e. Shaybānī] means that the territory was not converted into the Territory of War because Muslims were still living there peacefully. This is in accordance with the view of Abū Ḥanīfah. If they hold sway over the city for a short span of time and soon after they are subjugated without their laws being enforced or their rules established there, no one from amongst them will be taken as captive.

121. If both the spouses apostatize and move away to the Territory of War along with a minor child of theirs and afterwards, they are all subjugated, the child will be treated as *fay*. But if the mother remains a Muslim in the Territory of Islam and only the father takes away the child, the child will not be treated as *fay*. This will be the case if the mother dies as a Muslim. And also, if the mother is a Christian or a *Guaranteed Citizen* (*Dhimmi*). And also if the father is a *Guaranteed Citizen* and breaks his covenant.

122. If a child is born to an apostate couple in the Territory of War and then a child is born to their child, after which the Muslims subjugate them all, their child will be forced to accept Islam but not the child's child.

Section: When a group of the *Guaranteed Citizens* break the covenant:

123. When a group of the *Guaranteed Citizens* (*Ahl al-Dhimmah*) break the covenant and gain ascendancy in a city, the law for them will be like the law of the apostates; however, the state shall have the right to enslave their males. But if they return to peace, reconciliation and [revival of] the Guarantee, it will be accepted from them on the condition that they will be liable to all the obligations they were liable to before breaking the covenant, such as *qisas* and other financial obligations. They will, however, not be liable for whatever they have done during the period of belligerency. The case of apostates in this regard is also like this.

124. When the *Guaranteed Citizens* break the covenant along with their women and move away to the Territory of War, after which they come back together to resume the Guarantee, they will be recognized as still having valid marriages. But if any of them leaves behind a Guaranteed wife, she will be treated to have been separated from him because of the separation of the territories. Likewise, if an apostate moves away to the Territory of War, leaving behind in the Territory of Islam his wife, who had apostatized along with him, the marriage bond (*'ismah*) between them will come to an end.

125. If the apostates get power and force in their area, which becomes *Territory of Disbelief* then they move away to the Territory of War and get some captives from there and also get properties of the Muslims and the *Guaranteed Citizens* and finally re-embrace Islam, all these will be recognized as theirs except in case of a freeman, a *Mudabbar*, a *Mukatab* or an Umm Walad was taken away from a Muslim or a *Guaranteed Citizen*; these must be set free. Also, if the people of the Territory of Islam have captured some property or made captives from among them during the war with them and distribute these among themselves by way of booty, nothing out of it will be returned to them.

126. If the apostates demand that they should be accepted as citizens guaranteed by the Muslims, this demand should not be acceded to. If they demand that a truce is made with them so that they may have time to think over their problems [and misgivings about Islam], there is no harm in doing so if it is good for the Muslims, and Muslims have no power to fight them. But if the Muslims have sufficient strength and force to fight them and the war is also better for them than the truce, they should fight. The Islamic state should not receive any tax or tribute from them during the truce; but if it receives any, it will not be unlawful.

127. No agreement of peace or Guarantee shall be accepted by the Polytheists of Arabia. They should, rather, be invited to accept Islam; if they accept Islam, well and good; otherwise, they should be executed, their women and children should be enslaved and should not be forced to embrace Islam. But the Scriptures (*Ahl al-Kitab*) of Arabia are like the Scriptures of other countries.

128. A group of [Muslim] people go out to fight against the Territory of War, and a party from amongst them apostatizes and secedes from the main army and fights on their own and meet the enemy on their own, now Muslims get some booty, and the apostates also get some booty from the polytheists, after which the apostates repent [and return to Islam] before coming back to the Territory of Islam, they will not share with the Muslims their booty and the Muslims will not share with them their acquisitions. But if they engage in a battle after this incident and all of them jointly take part in it, they all will share each other's acquisitions.

129. There is no liability on a person who kills the apostates before inviting them to Islam.

130. If an adolescent boy apostatizes from Islam, he will not be executed. If he reaches puberty while still a disbeliever, I [Shaybānī] would prefer to detain him and would not execute him. Analogical reasoning requires that his apostasy before puberty should be null and void. But if an adolescent Magian boy who is grown up with some understanding but who has not yet reached puberty embraces Islam, he will be treated as a Muslim according to the opinion of all of them. However, Abu Yusuf reviewed his opinion afterwards and said: "His Islam will be accepted as Islam but his *Kufr* (disbelief) will not be treated as *Kufr*.

131. When an apostate repents but again returns to his apostasy and again embraces Islam, I will accept it from him even though it is repeated many times. The apostasy committed by an intoxicated person is nothing according to the juristic preference or *Istihsan*. When the heirs of an apostate demand that his personal belongings earned by him during the period of his apostasy should be given to

them on the plea that he had re-embraced Islam before his death, they will be required to produce evidence to prove this statement. On the other hand, Abu Yusuf and Muhammad [ibn al-Hasan al-Shaybānī] are of the view that the personal belongings of an apostate shall be inherited from him like his other property.

Section: When A Case breaks the covenant.

132. When a *Guaranteed Citizen* (*Dhimmi*) breaks the covenant and moves away to the Territory of War, his heirs shall deal with his bequests in the same manner as the bequests of an apostate are dealt with.

****

Chapter VIII : The Rebels

Section: Some virtues of 'Ali (may Allah be pleased with him)

133. He [Shaybānī] has mentioned on the authority of his chain of narrators that Kuthayyir al-Hadrami entered the mosque of Kufah. Suddenly, he noticed that a band of people were abusing and vilifying Ali. Among them was a man wearing a burnoose who was saying: "I swear by Allah I must kill him". Kuthayyir says: "I caught him and took him to 'Ali. I told 'Ali: 'I heard this man swearing by Allah to kill you'. 'Alī said to the man: Come nearer. Woe unto you, who are you? He answered: I am Sawar al-Minqarī. 'Alī, then said to me: 'Let him go'. I said, 'How can I let him go while he has already sworn by Allah to kill you?' 'Ali said, 'But how can I kill him when he has not yet killed me?' I, then, said: 'But he has also abused you!'. 'Ali said; 'Well! you may also abuse him if you like or just set him free'.

134. It has been reported to us from 'Ali (may Allah be pleased with him) that he said on the day [of the battle] of the Camel: "Do not pursue the retreater, do not execute the prisoner, do not kill the wounded; no veil should be opened [i.e.,, no women should be molested or made captive], and no property should be taken".

135. He [Shaybānī] says: "When the *people of justice* defeat the *People of rebellion* it is not suitable for the *People of justice* to pursue a retreater, to execute a prisoner or to kill a wounded person, provided they have no troops to return to [in order to regain strength]. But if they have some troops to return to [in order to

regain strength], then their prisoners may be executed, their retreaters may be pursued and their wounded may be killed.

136. Whatever the *People of justice* acquire out of the beasts of burden and weaponry of the *People of rebellion*, it may lawfully be used against them; but as soon as the war comes to an end, all this must be returned to them. Their acquired property will also be returned to them.

137. It has been reported to us from 'Ali ibn Abi Talib (may Allah be pleased with him) that he had thrown whatever his army had taken from the army of the People of Nahrawan's onto an open ground: Whoever recognized his property took it; the last thing to be recognized as belonging to somebody was a cooking pot of steel, and he took it.

138. If a belligerent woman from the *People of Rebellion* is caught fighting, she will be detained till such time when nobody from amongst them remains [in the battlefield]. But she shall not be executed. If a free man or a slave is found fighting in the army of the *People of rebellion,* he may be killed. But if a slave is there only to serve his master without doing any fighting he will be detained till such time when nobody remains [in the battlefield] but he will not be executed.

139. As to the beasts of burden and weaponry acquired by the Muslims which they are not in an immediate need to use, Shaybānī says, the beasts of burden shall be sold and their price shall be retained to be returned along with the weaponry to their owners after the war comes to an end.

140. If the *People of rebellion* demand truce [with the Muslims], it may be accepted if it is good for the Muslims; but nothing shall be taken from them against it. As soon as the *People of rebellion* repent and enter into normal relations with the *People of justice,* they will not be liable to anything done or taken by them. However, if something is found intact it will be returned to its owner. Likewise, the things done or taken by the *People of justice* [will only be returned to their original owners if the corpus of the property is found intact]. If the *People of rebellion* seek assistance and help from a group of the *Guaranteed Citizens* in their fight [against the *People of justice*], this assistance will not be treated to be a violation of the Covenant [on the part of the *Guaranteed Citizens*], even if they fight along with them. Their position in respect of what they acquire or commit in the Territory of War shall be like that of the *People of rebellion.*

141. It is advisable for the *People of justice* when they face the *People of rebellion* to invite them first to accept the just [and legitimate] authority; it is good to do that, but if they did not do it, there is no liability on them. If they [i.e., *People of justice*] shoot them with arrows and mangonel, it will not be objectionable. Also, they may release water or fire against them. There is also no objection if they undertake a night ambush against them.

142. If a truce takes place between them [i.e. between the *People of justice* and the *People of rebellion*) and both the parties deposit some hostages with each other on the condition that whoever commits treachery, the blood of their hostages will be lawful for the other party to shed [i.e., to kill them] and the *People of rebellion* commit treachery and kill the hostages in their custody, it will not be advisable for the *People of justice* to kill the hostages in their custody. They may, however, detain them till such time when they either

become Muslims or accept the guaranteed status in the Islamic State.

143. If a person from amongst the *People of justice* gives a quarter to a person from amongst the *People of rebellion*, this quarter will be valid. The same will be the case if he says: "I have no way over you" or "There is no objection against you". And also, if he says this in some other language. And also, if it is done by a woman. But if the quarter is given by a slave not fighting along with his master, it will not be valid; however, if he is fighting, his quarter will be valid both for the non-Muslims as well as for the *People of rebellion*. The quarter given by a *Guaranteed Citizen* present in the Muslim Camp is not valid, whether fighting or not.

144. If the women of the camp of the *People of Rebellion actually fight against the People of Justice*, the latter may also be allowed to fight against them. But if the women are not actually fighting, the *People of justice* are not permitted to fight them.

145. If a group of the *People of justice* are in the hands of the *People of rebellion* as traders or as prisoners where some of them commit criminal acts against the others, no *Qisas* will be liable against each other on the victory of the *People of justice* because these acts were committed [in an area and at a time] when the Law was not applicable. In such situations courts may also not act upon the written records of the courts established by the *People of rebellion*.

Section: Records of the courts of the People of rebellion are not admissible.

146. If the *People of rebellion* gain ascendancy over a city and appoint a Qadi from amongst the inhabitants of the city, but he is not one of the rebels, he shall establish the prescribed punishments, execute the visas and enforce the Law of Islam among the people with full justice and truth. He shall have no option except this. If he writes or sends a document to the Qadi of the *People of justice* about the right of a citizen of the city along with the details of the evidence of the witnesses who have given evidence in favor of the person concerned, he [i.e. the Qadi of the *People of justice*] shall validate the judgement, provided the Qadi to whom this letter is written or document sent knows the witnesses who have given evidence before that Qadi, and they [i.e., the witnesses] are not from amongst the *People of rebellion*. But if he does not know them, then I [i.e., Shaybānī] do not think that he should accept this document as valid.

147. Whatever the *People of rebellion* commit or acquire, such as murder or appropriation of property, etc., before they go out on rebellion or fighting, it will not be valid to make any agreement of peace with them on the condition that all their liabilities be waived. They will be liable for all their commissions, such as Qisas, compensation, etc.

148. The dead bodies of those killed from amongst the *People of justice* should be treated in the same manner in which the dead bodies of the martyrs are treated. 159 No funeral prayer should be offered for the dead of the *People of Rebellion*; they should simply be buried. I disapprove that their heads be chopped off and be carried around here and there because this act amounts to mutilating the body. It has been reported to us from 'Ali ibn Abi Talib (may Allah be pleased with him) that he treated [the dead bodies of the *People of rebellion*] in this manner in all his battles.

149. When a soldier of the *People of Justice kills his own rebel father [on the battlefield],* he will still inherit him. Likewise, if the rebel [father] kills him he will also inherit him according to Abū Ḥanīfah and Muhammad [al-Shaybānī]; because he has killed him on the basis of *Ta'wil* [Interpretation of the Divine Text.]. But Abu Yusuf says that he [i.e., the rebel father] will not inherit his son. It is detestable for a soldier of the *People of Justice to kill his own father or brother who is in the camp of the People of Rebellion.* Likewise, it is detestable for a Muslim son to kill his non-Muslim father [on the battlefield]. But it is not detestable for him to kill his own non-Muslim brother, paternal uncle or maternal uncle. But if the non-Muslim father attacks him in order to kill him, the son may defend himself and keep on fighting. If a person from amongst the *People of justice* happens to be in the camp of the *People of rebellion* where someone kills him, he [i.e., the killer] will not be liable to pay the *Diyah* because it is absolutely permissible to fight the *People of rebellion.*

150. If a rebel enters the camp of the *People of Justice* with a permission of security and a person from amongst the *People of Justice* kills him, he shall be liable to pay the *Diyah.* When a soldier from the *People of justice* attacks a rebel in a military encounter and the latter says "I have repented" and throws away the arms, the soldier from the *People of justice* must immediately cease fighting. And also, if the rebel says: "Desist from me so that I may ponder over this matter and I may afterwards follow you" and throws away the arms. But if he says without throwing away the arms: "I follow your religion", he [Shaybānī] says that he is right in saying this because he really follows that religion; but in this case the soldier from the *People of justice* should not stop fighting.

151. When a group of the *People of rebellion* gain ascendancy in a city and, later another group of the *People of rebellion* fight the former, defeat them and try to enslave the women and children of the inhabitants of the city, the inhabitants of the city have no choice except to fight in defense of women and children.

152. If the *People of rebellion* enter into an agreement of truce (*Muwada'ah*) or friendship with a group of people from the Territory of War, it is not advisable for the *People of justice* to fight against the latter.161 If the *People of rebellion* commit treachery against these [people of the Territory of War] and enslave them, the *People of justice* should not buy these slaves from them because those who had entered into the agreement of truce with them were Muslims [therefore all Muslims must honor that agreement]. Whenever the *People of rebellion* repent, these [enslaved prisoners] should be returned to the *People of war*. The same should be done when the agreement of truce is made by the *People of justice*. There is no harm if the *People of justice* seek cooperation and help from a group of the *People of rebellion* or that of the *Guaranteed People* against the *Khawarij* provided the Law of Justice remains supreme.

153. If the *People of rebellion* have no power and strength and only one or two persons have come out from a city or town on the plea of some [wrong] interpretation or Ta'wil [of the Qur'an or the Sunnah], who fight and then seek a permission of security, they shall be answerable for all their actions according to the Law. Their position will be that of highwaymen, If a person assaults another person within the town with a stick or a stone and the victim kills the offender with an iron weapon he (the killer) shall be liable to *qisaṣ* according to Abū Ḥanīfah. But Abu Yusuf and Muhammad [ibn al-Hasan al-Shaybānī] say: "If the offender had assaulted him with

something which could kill a person and the victim kills him in defense, his [i.e., the offender's] blood will not be protected by law. In such a situation, a victim may advisably kill an offender. If the offender draws weapons against a person who kills him [in self-defense] he shall not be liable for anything.

154. If a person raids another person in his house during the night and steals his belongings while overpowering him with a weapon or stick and the master of the house kills him and later produces evidence to this effect, he shall not be liable to anything. Same will be the case if a raider overpowers a person with a weapon in daytime. But if he overpowers him in a daytime without any weapon and the master of the house kills him, his *'Aqilahs* shall be liable to pay the *Diyah*. If the victim kills the offender with a weapon, he will be liable to *qisas*. So also, in cases of intentional murder instead of murders in all these situations, [there shall be liability to *qisas*].

155. If a group of people commit highway robbery and waylay the travelers without use of weapons and the latter kill the bandits, they shall not be liable to anything. But if someone quarrels with another person inside a city without any weapon and the latter kills him, he shall be liable to *qisas*, if he kills him with a weapon. This is because he was more capable of seeking help from other people [than the one who didn't have any weapon]. If a group of bandits or men like them gain ascendancy over a city without having [any basis whatsoever from] some interpretation [of the Qur'an or the Sunnah], kill people and take away their property and are eventually subjugated, they shall be liable for all their acts.

Section: Validity of the judgement of the Qādī appointed by the *People of rebellion.*

156. If the *People of rebellion* gain ascendancy over a town, appoint a Qadi there and he decides cases, and later, the *People of justice* regain control of the town and the decisions of the Qadi are submitted to the Qadi of the *People of justice*, he should enforce only such decisions of his as are based on justice, are legitimate and are in accordance with the views of any of the [recognized] jurists.

157. If the *People of justice* and the *People of rebellion* jointly fight against the *people of war* and get some booty, they both shall share it and the one fifth shall go to the *People of justice*. Likewise, if one of these two groups gets booty to the exclusion of the other, they both shall share it. Likewise, if the *Imam* [Head of the Islamic State] fights along with a Muslim army and he dies in the Territory of War and the army is divided on the issue of succession, after which the whole army or a group of them gets some booty, they all shall share it.

158. If a group of soldiers go out from a town for fighting without the permission of the *Imam* [i.e., Central Muslim Authority] and get some booty, the one-fifth thereof shall be taken and the rest shall be distributed among them. This situation is different from the one in which one or two persons go out.

159. If a group of the *People of rebellion* seek help from a group of the *People of war* and these latter attack the *People of justice* and fighting ensues and eventually the *People of justice* subjugate them, they may enslave these *People of war*. The fact that the *People of rebellion* had sought their help shall not be considered to be a permission of security for them. Likewise, if the *People of rebellion* enter into an

agreement of Muwada'ah [truce, armistice or friendship] with a group of the *people of war,* and these latter attack the *People of justice* and fighting ensues, and eventually the *People of justice* subjugate them, they may enslave them.

160. Whoever joins the camp of the *People of rebellion* and fights along with them, he will not be treated as an apostate, his property will not be distributed among his heirs, and the *Ismah* [bond of marriage] between him and his wife shall not be treated to have come to an end.

Chapter IX:
Another chapter on Booty

161. Abū Ḥanīfah (may Allah have mercy on him) has said: "A volunteer in a war and a regular enrolled warrior are equal in their entitlement to the booty". A person who enters the Territory of War for trade and commerce and happens to be in the Muslim camp shall not be entitled to the booty [merely because of his presence there]. However, if the Muslims meet the enemy and that person fights along with them, he shall have a share in the booty.

Section: Six questions answered by Abū Ḥanīfah.

162. He [Shaybānī) says: "I asked Abū Ḥanīfah about the killing of women, children, such old men who do not have the ability to fight, those suffering from chronic illness and are unable fight. He forbade their killing and detested it. I asked him about the killing of monks, residents of hermitages and cross-strip-wearers. He thought their killing [in the battlefield] was good and he disliked that they should be spared. I further asked him about a person who makes an individual from the enemy captive, can he kill him or must he bring him to the *Imam* [the Leader]? He answered: "Whichever of the two he does is good". But according to Abu Yusuf and Muhammad, he should do whatever is best for the Muslims. I again asked him about the dead body of a person from amongst the *People of war* killed by the Muslims: can the Muslims demand a price of his dead body from the *People of war*? He answered: "There is no objection in doing so in

the Territory of War outside the Muslim camp. Don't you see that it is permissible for the Muslims to seize their property by force? Now, when they are willingly prepared to pay, it will be permissible". But Abu Yusuf says: "I detest it and forbid it. It is not allowed for the Muslims to sell the dead corpses and the pigs and swine or to receive usury from the *People of war* or from anybody else". I also asked him about Muslims seeking help and cooperation from non-Muslims against the *People of war*. He replied: "There is no harm in it, provided the Law of Islam remains supreme and overpowering. These people [i.e., cooperating non-Muslims] may also be given something from the booty". I also asked him about a prisoner, should he be executed or ransomed? He said: "He should not be ransomed but should either be killed or be declared as *Fay*, whichever of the two is better for the Muslims should be done by the *Imam* [the Government]".

163. Abū Ḥanīfah has said: There is no harm if the Muslim prisoners are ransomed for non-Muslim prisoners. He used to dislike their ransom for cash-payment.

164. Abū Ḥanīfah further said: If the riding animal of a Muslim runs away to them [i.e., non-Muslims] and they capture it in their own territory and, then, the Muslims conquer that territory, the owner of the animal may take it without any price before distribution [of the booty] and with price after the distribution. According to Abū Ḥanīfah, the case of a fleeing animal is different from that of a fleeing slave.

165. Abū Ḥanīfah further said: If a person from amongst the non-Muslims comes out [to the Territory of Islam] with a permission of security along with some property originally belonging to a Muslim and he [i.e., non-Muslim alien] sells it in the Territory of Islam, no

one shall have any right to snatch it from him, according to the view of all the jurists. However, in case of a fleeing slave, Abū Ḥanīfah says that his master may take him into his possession wherever he finds him without paying any price.

166. If the non-Muslims take a Muslim (slave-girl] as captive and take her into their safe custody, then a Muslim purchased her from them and she becomes blind while with him, her master shall be entitled to take her back only after paying her full price, according to the opinion of Abū Yusuf and Muhammad who has also said: "this is the view of Abū Ḥanīfah as far as I know". Likewise, if her hand is chopped off and the purchaser has received its Arsh, her master can take her back only after paying her full original price in disregard of the Arsh. Likewise, if the purchaser gouges out her eye. So also, if she gives birth to a child while in the custody of the purchaser and he manumits either of the two: the mother or the child, the master may take the other [i.e., non- manumitted of the two] after paying full price. Likewise, if the child is killed and the purchaser has received his Arsh, the master can take the mother on payment of full price.

167. If a person sells his slave-girl to another person but the purchaser neither takes possession of the slave-girl nor pays the price in cash and in the meantime the enemy takes her as captive and a person purchases her from them, this purchaser shall have no claim over her until the first seller [exercises his right to] take her on payment of two prices: the first price on which he had purchased her and the [second] price on which he has to secure her redemption.

Section: All freemen taken prisoners by the enemy shall be considered free as soon as the enemy enters the fold of Islam.

168. Every freeman taken as captive by the enemy shall be considered free on the entry of the enemy into the fold of Islam provided the captive is still in his possession. Likewise, a *Mudabbar*, a *Mukātab* and an *Umm Walad* shall be treated as they were before. Every ownership which is not saleable cannot be owned by the *People of war*. If a person directs another person to purchase these slaves from them [i.e., the *people of war*], the purchaser shall have the right to demand the payment of the price he has paid to be reimbursed to him by them. The same is the case with the *Mukatab*. As to the *Mudabbar* and the *Umm Walad*, their purchaser shall have the right to demand their price from themselves on their manumission. In case he had purchased them without being asked to do that, he will not have any title to their ownership and his property [paid as a price] will go waste.

169. If a person directs another person to purchase a freeman from the Territory of War and he identifies a particular person to him and he purchases that person, the person so purchased shall not be responsible to repay the price the purchaser has paid. However, the person so directed shall have the right to recover his money from the person who had directed him to do so, provided the latter had guaranteed the payment of price or had asked the man to purchase for himself [i.e., for the person directing]. But if he had said: "Purchase him for yourself and give him [to me] as charity", he will not be liable to pay any compensation.

170. If the non-Muslims make the slave of a Muslim captive and then another Muslim purchases that slave from them and mortgages him, his first master shall have no right to take him back without redeeming him. If he wishes to pay the debt voluntarily and then pay the price he may do so. He will be treated as a volunteer in the payment of the debt and the master shall not be forced to redeem the mortgage. If he had given him on rent for some period of time, the master can take him back on the payment of price and cancel the remaining period of rent because a contract of rent can be terminated because of some valid excuse.

171. If a group of the *People of war* gain ascendancy over another group of the *People of war* and the former make the latter slaves of their king and, thereafter, the king and his countrymen embrace Islam, these conquered people shall be recognized to be his slaves and he shall have the right to dispose them of as he likes. As to his army with the help of which he had conquered them, they shall be considered to be freemen. If the king passes away and his property is inherited by some of his children to the exclusion of others, or he himself had assigned a particular area to each one of them, it will be accepted as a valid arrangement if he had done it before accepting Islam or the Guarantee (*Dhimmah*) and it was only after this that his son(s) have accepted Islam. If he had made this arrangement at a time when he was party to an agreement of truce [with the Muslims], it will be accepted as valid. So also, if he had assigned his wealth to one of his sons but another son of his inherited it afterwards who either kills the original inheritor or banishes him and captures all his possessions and then enters the fold of Islam, this son shall be recognized to be the owner of all his possessions. But if this son does all this after the defeated son has already

accepted Islam or the Guarantee, he will be restored to the possession of all this property and his brother will be expelled from that property. This step will be taken only when the former brother had taken possession of the property in a state of being a Muslim or a *Guaranteed Citizen*. But if he was in possession of this property in a state of being a belligerent and then accepts Islam or the Guarantee, all his possessions will be acknowledged as his property.

172. If the Muslims conquer that area, all this property shall be restored to the first son without any price if he comes before its distribution [as booty among the warriors], and on payment of price if he comes after the distribution. If the Muslims do not conquer it but only purchase the property from them, they can do so and the first son shall have the right to take this property on payment of price. If this son has done this when both of them were Muslims or *Dhimmis*, it will not be permissible for him to claim the property and the Muslims shall have no right to purchase from him anything appropriated by him. In case someone purchases anything from this property, the first son shall have the right to claim it without any price. If this capturing son becomes an apostate after capturing the estate, fortifies the arca and enforces the laws of Polytheism and, then, the Muslims regain ascendancy over it, the overpowered son shall have the right to take whatever he finds intact out of his property without any consideration before its distribution and on payment of price after the distribution. And Allah knows best.

****

Notes and references

1. The word A'rab al-Muslimin has been used in the original which literally means Muslim bedouins or Muslim desert-dwellers. Here the term refers to those Muslim bedouins who preferred to live in their own areas and did not choose to settle down in Madinah as many other migrants did. In those days the Holy Prophet (peace be upon him) required of every believer to migrate to Madinah where the nascent Muslim community was in need of greater manpower to protect itself from the onslaught of the surrounding hostile tribes. After the conquest of Makkah, this requirement was relaxed. See, for further details, Muhanumad Hamidullah, Ahd-i Nabawi Mén Nizām-i Hukmrāni (Karachi, 1981), pp. 262-283.
2. *Fay'* means proceeds of the state from the enemy property other than war booty.
3. Protection tax paid by the non-Muslim citizens to the Islamic state in consideration of the protection provided to them by the state and in lieu of conscription. For details see Muhammad Hamidullah, Muslim Conduct of State (Lahore, 1987), pp. 104, 117, 171, 172, 241, 244.
4. According to Abu Yusuf, these directions were given when the Holy Prophet (peace be upon him) was still in the early years of his career in Madinah. The law of Islam regarding warfare and international relations was yet to take a final shape and many of its commandments were yet to be revealed. In that situation it was quite possible that something might be committed in the name of Allah and His Messenger without their having said or ordered it.

5. In the text, the word *ayyim* has been used which means any adult person who has no spouse, whether unmarried, widow, widower, divorcee etc. The reference in the text is to the difference of opinion about the management of the property allocated to the Holy Prophet (peace be upon him) as a part of *Khums*. 'Umar thought that it should be administered by the successor of the Holy Prophet (peace be upon him) in office while some of his family members, particularly 'Ali and Ibn Abbas, in the beginning, were of the view that its administration be handed over to the Prophet's family. But it is significant that during his own caliphate 'Ali did not change the practice followed since the days of Abi Bakr and 'Umar Abu Ja'far has referred to its reason in para 3 above.
6. A battle between the Muslims and Jews in 5 AH.
7. Ignorance or *Jahiliyyah* is a term given by the Qur'an to the un-Islamic state of affairs prevalent before the revelation of the Qur'an. Some recent scholars (e.g., Sayyid Qutb) have given a wider meaning to the term. They use it for a cultural and civilizational pattern different from that of Islam. To these scholars, the Jahiliyyah of pre-Islamic Arabia was only a *jahiliyyah* but not the *Jahiliyyah*.
8. This ruling of the Holy Prophet (peace be upon him) lays down the principle that acquisition of enemy property in war is a legitimate mode of the transfer of the ownership of a property.
9. The area situated in the delta of Euphrates and Tigris was known as the Sawad or black area for its dark greenery.
10. Najdah ibn 'Amir al-Hanafi, a *Khāriji* leader after whom the Najdah group of the Khawarij is named. The fact that the *Khariji* leaders used to refer important religio-legal matters to

the Companions of the Holy Prophet for rulings and guidance throws light on their hitherto misunderstood conduct and relationship with the mainstream.

11. i.e., the share of the household (of the Prophet) as mentioned in the Qur'an 8:41.
12. Muhammad ibn Ishaq (d. 150 AH), one of the earliest biographers of the Holy Prophet (peace be upon him), whose findings have been preserved partly by his illustrious follower and disciple, Ibn Hisham. His own work on the life of the Holy Prophet has been recently discovered in Morocco and has been published there. An Urdu translation has also appeared. See Muhammad Tu*fay*l, Nugush, Seerat Number, (Lahore, 1985), pp. 8-395.
13. Al-Kalbi, Muhammad ibn al-Sa'ib (d. 151 AH), a historian of note who is not considered much reliable by the traditionists. See 31 below.
14. Shaybānī has given all this evidence in order to establish that the booty should not be distributed among the warriors in the enemy's territory; it should first be brought to the Islamic territory and then it should be distributed. The principle underlying this discussion is that legitimate transfer of ownership of the enemy property takes place only after total and complete physical possession of the property of the enemy in a lawful war. Now, the total possession can only materialize when the property is safely brought to the Islamic territory.
15. As mentioned in the Qur'an 8:41. The question was as to how this share is to be disposed of after the demise of the Holy Prophet (peace be on him). There were different views among the jurists about its disposal after the demise of the Holy

Prophet. According to one opinion, this will continue to be admissible to the relatives of the Holy Prophet. According to another opinion, it will now be the right of the relatives of the successor of the Holy Prophet in office. According to yet another opinion, (mentioned in the text, para 14), its disposal may be made according to the contingencies of time as was done by Abu Bakr.

16. In the text the word *qa'id*has been used. *Qa'id* literally means one who is sitting, i.e., the one who sits at home and does not go out the *jihad.*
17. In the text the word *shakhis* has been used. *Shakhis* literally means one who goes out, i.e., one who goes out to take part in the *Jihad.*
18. Should not irrigate other's crops with his water. This phrase metaphorically means that a man should in no case have sexual relations with any woman who is or believed to be pregnant from another man. However, to marry a woman who is pregnant from an illicit intercourse is allowed but before having conjugal relations with her, the husband should wait till the birth of the child. This instruction was given by the Holy Prophet (peace be on him) at the time of war to prevent Muslim soldiers from having relations with newly purchased female slaves before the passage of the waiting period which is intended to ensure the emptiness of the 'land' from the 'crops' of someone else.
19. The term *Fay*' has been taken from the Qur'anic verses 59:6-10 to denote a kind of income in which the property of the enemy accrues to the Muslims without warlike operations. The Qur'an lays down the rule that the *fay*' property would go to the public exchequer and should not be distributed among

the warriors like normal war booty. *Fay'* is to be spent for welfare purposes. See, for a brief economic discussion on the concept and practice of *fay*, Muhammad Yusufuddin, *Islam ké Ma'ashi Nazariyye* (Karachi, 1984), vol. II, pp. 601-645; also, Nicolas P. Aghnides, *An Introduction to Mohammedan Theories of Finance* (Lahore, 1981), (reprint), pp. 425-433.

20. There is difference of opinion among the jurists about the killing of women. Basing on aḥadīth such as the one quoted in the text, Abū Ḥanīfah prohibits the killing of women in all situations. But other jurists, specially Shafi'ī, differentiate between various situations and prescribe different rules for different situations. See, for a typical discussion, Kasani, *Bada'i' al-Sana'i'* (Karachi, 1400 AH), vol. VII, pp. 101-102.
21. Choice or *safi* was the traditional prerogative of the commander of the victorious army who could select any one item for his personal use out of the booty before its distribution. For a juristic discussion on safi see Sarakhsī. *Sharh al-Siyar al-Kabir* (Afghanistan edition, 1405 AH), vol. II, pp. 607-619.
22. Amir ibn Sharahil al-Sha'bi (d. 104AH/722C.E) was a prominent jurist and traditionist of Kufah. His narrations from 'Ali ibn Abi Talib have been a subject of much discussion among the traditionists. While some tend to accept them as authentic, others doubt his direct association with 'Ali. This difference of opinion caused other differences on some juridical issues about which the opinion is based on Sha'bi's narrations from 'Ali.
23. In the manuscripts before us, we have deciphered the word here as Nujayr. See Yaqut al-Hamawi, *Mu'jam al-Buldan*, (Beirut, 1984), vol. V., pp. 272-274.

24. It has been a subject of intense discussion among the early jurists of Islam whether non-Muslims should be involved in the wars of *Jihad* fought by the Muslims against other non-Muslim powers. The *Jihad* being primarily a war waged for the cause of Islam, non-Muslim citizens of the Islamic state were exempted by some jurists from participation in it. Other jurists have viewed this question differently and have held that a non-Muslim citizen or ally of the Islamic state can be included in the Muslim army provided the supremacy of the rule of the Shari'ah is guaranteed. Both the groups have, however, based their arguments on the sayings of the Holy Prophet on different occasions and in different contexts. Shaybānī seems to tend to the view that non-Muslims' participation in *Jihad* should be discouraged as a rule and should only be allowed in exceptional cases.
25. In the original the word *mudd* has been used. It was a measure equal to 1.032 liters or 815.39 grams according to the Hanafis and 543 granis or 0.687 liters according to others, specially the three Imams.
26. Hasan ibn Yasar al-Baṣrī (d. 110 AH/728 CE), perhaps the most celebrated scholar among the Successors (Tabi'un), was widely respected for his scholarship, piety and courage to speak the truth in the face of the rulers.
27. 'Ata' ibn Abi Rabah, (d. 114 AH/732 CE), a great jurist, a Successor who was acknowledged as the mufti and the *muhaddith* of Makkah.
28. Abu Yusuf and most of the Hanafis do not agree with the view that a non-Muslim prisoner of war may be ransomed. According to them, a stern and harsh attitude should be

adopted towards the enemy soldiers taken captives in the battle-field.

29. The original words are *adnahum* which literally means: their lowest, their most inferior, their nearest, etc. But here it means that the commitment made to the enemy by a common soldier will have to be honored by the rest of the Muslims.
30. By mentioning this report the author wants to establish that warlike operations may be initiated in the sacred months. Such acts were previously held by the Arabs to be forbidden during the months of Muharram, Rajab, Dhu'l-Qa'dah and Dhu'l-Hijjah. The sub-heading given to the next paragraph by one of the scribes further clarifies this position.
31. Kalbi, Muḥammad ibn al-Sa'ib, Abu'l-Nadr (d. 146 AH/CE 763), was a Kufi scholar who left his impact as a historian and exegete. Although a celebrated authority in the fields of *Tafsir* and history of pre-Islamic and early Islamic Arabia, he was not considered a reliable source of Hadith by several doctors of this discipline, presumably because of his Shiite leanings. See Ibn Hajar, *Tahdhib al-Tahdhib*, vol. IX, p. 178; Ton Khallikan, *Wafayat al-A'yan*, vol. I, p. 493; Dhahabi, *Mizan al-I'tidal*, vol. III, p. 61.
32. It has been a unanimous view of the Muslim jurists that the primary objective of *Jihad* is to remove hindrances in the way of disseminating the message of Islam and to weaken the forces that come in its way. Thus, the ultimate purpose of *jihad* is moral. spiritual and ideological and not political or military. Therefore, it has always been considered necessary to invite the opponent to accept Islam before starting any war- like operation. This invitation, on the one hand, reminds

the Muslim warriors that their purpose is not to gain material benefits and, on the other, gives an opportunity to the opponent to end hostilities at once and to enter the fraternity of Islam.

33. We have translated the terms *Dar al-Islam* and *Dar al-Harb* as the Territory of Islam and the Territory of War respectively. In the early stages of the formative phase of *Fiqh,* the Muslim empire happened to be virtually at war with all its important neighbors. The international intercourse between Muslim state and other states was either in the nature of a hostile relationship or that of political and military submission to the Muslim power. In such a situation, Muslim jurists divided the territories around them into the Territory of Islam where the laws of Islam were supreme and the Territory of War which included all the areas at war with them. As to the regions and countries recognizing the political supremacy and military superiority of the Muslim Empire but retaining their legal and religious autonomy, they were treated as a part of the Territories of Islam by the Hanafis and were called by others as *Territory of Peace, Territory of Truce and Territory of Covenant* (*Dar al-Sulḥ, Dār al-Amn, and Dar al-'Ahd* respectively).

34. 'Full possession' is the translation of the term *ihraz* which literally means acquisition, preservation, protection, taking into custody, taking care of and fortification. In Muslim municipal and international law, *ihrāz* is a mode of acquisition of property recognized as a valid source of ownership. According to the law of Islam, anybody who takes into his custody an unowned or free property (*mubah*) is recognized as its lawful owner. The legitimacy of the ownership of hunted animals, for example, is based on the principle of

iḥraz. The property of the people of the Territory of War is considered to be a free property as long as they are at war with the Muslims. As such any Muslim soldier who takes it into custody during the hostilities and secures it to the Territory of Islam is accepted as its rightful owner. Likewise, a non-Muslim belligerent who acquires the property of a Muslim to the Territory of War during hostilities will also be accepted as its rightful owner.

35. We have preferred here the word 'Government' for the translation of the Term Imam which literally means a leader or guide. But it is used in the legal literature of Islam for a Muslim head of the state and head of the Government as well as for the Islamic government as an institution. We have translated it differently on different occasions according to the requirements of the context.

36. The question of the permissibility or otherwise of the distribution of war- booty while the army is still in the enemy territory has been a subject of extensive discussion in the early writings on the subject. Abū Ḥanifah, Awza'ī, Shaf'i and Abu Yusuf, all the great jurists of the second century of Hijrah, addressed themselves to this question. This discussion acquired significance as it answered another more important legal question: how and when does a victorious army gain lawful title to the property obtained from the enemy during the battle. According to Abū Ḥanīfah, *ihraz* (taking into safe custody of a free property) is the cause of the transfer of the title and *iḥraz* becomes perfect only when the victorious army succeeds in taking the property so acquired to its own territory in a safe and secure condition. According to Abū Ḥanīfah, this principle applies to both Muslim and non-

Muslim armies. But Awza'i does not agree with this principle and he is supported by Shafi'ī in his logic that a Muslim army becomes the owner of an enemy property as soon as it able to lay hand on it. Both rely on various incidents reported from the days of the Holy Prophet (peace be on him). For details, see Shafi'ī, Kitab al-Umm (Beirut, 1973), vol. VII, pp. 333-336, and Abu Yusuf, al- Radd *'Ala Siyar al-Awza'i* (Cairo, n.d.), pp. 1-12. See also other major works on *Fiqh*, chapters on Siyar, in loco.

37. The same principle of *iḥraz* applies here.
38. As a general principle, the Qur'an (2:205) prohibits the destruction of life and agriculture but in cases of extreme necessity where it is inevitable for defense and military purposes to destroy the enemy property, it is allowed to do so. This permission is based on the Qur'anic verse 59:5.
39. The original word used in the text for 'government' is Imam, literally a leader or guide, which primarily means head of the state or the commander of the faithful. But Muslim jurists have generally used this term in an impersonal way to connote the sense of the office or the authority of the head of the state. We have, therefore, preferred here the term 'Government' rather than "Head of the State".
40. *Kharaj* was a land revenue levied on the lands owned by the state and cultivated by the tenants. It was levied either on the lands conquered by the Islamic state or on the land acceded to the Islamic state as a result of some treaty providing for this levy. There were mainly two kinds of *kharaj*: wazifah and muqasamah, the former being a specific amount to be paid by the tenant while the latter being a predetermined ratio to be

paid as such out of the total produce. See, for details, inter alia, *Diya' al-Din al-Rayyis, al-Kharaj fi'l-Dawlah al-Islamiyyah.*

41. This rule is again based on the principle of *Ihraz.* In this case the enemy property can only be considered to be the lawful booty of the Muslim army after it is taken out of the enemy territory and is safely taken to the Territory of Islam. Now, all those who have participated in the process of *ihraz* i.e., safely taking the booty into the Territory of Islam will be entitled to have a share in it.
42. *Dhimmi,* literally guaranteed, protected or covenanted, means a non- Muslim citizen of the Islamic state whose area of residence has been acceded to the Islamic state as a result of military conquest. For details see Ibn Qayyim al- Jawziyyah, *Ahkam Ahl al- Dhimmah,* ed. by Subhi al- Ṣāliḥ (Beirut, 1981), 2 volumes.
43. Mukatab, literally a party to a written document, means a slave with whom his master has made an agreement to manumit him on the payment of certain amount as his price. Such an agreement was normally written and hence the terms *Mukatab* and *Kitabah.* See for details any standard compendium on Fiqh, chapters on *Mukātab* or *Kitābah.*
44. The word "... belonging" has been used for the term Salab occured in the text. Literally, spoil, plunder or booty, salab technically means whatever is seized or carried off by force from the body or possession of an overpowered or killed enemy soldier such as his clothing, weapons, beast, money in his possession, etc.
45. *Istiḥsan,* literally approval, expression of pleasure and consent or the selection of the best part or alternative, technically means juristic preference by a jurist in a case where a rule

based on the strict application of the principle of *qiyas* or analogical reasoning to a situation turns out to be in conflict with an established principle or violates the spirit of the law. Sometimes "it may happen that the law analogically deduced fails to commend itself to the jurist, owing to its narrowness and in-adaptability to the habits and usages of the people and being likely to cause hardships and inconveniences. In that event also according to the Hanfis, a jurist is at liberty to refuse (sic) to adopt the law to which analogy points, and to accept instead a rule which in his opinion would better advance the welfare of men and the interest of justice". Abdur Rahim, The Principles of Muhammadan Jurisprudence (Lahore, n.d.), pp. 163-166. See also, for a modern exposition of the principle of *Istihsan*, Aḥmad Hasan, Analogical Reasoning in Islamic Jurisprudence (Islamabad, 1986), pp. 409-424. This process, which is known as *istihsan*, is similar, at least in its purpose, to equity in the Anglo-Saxon tradition.

46. While commenting on this rule, Sarakhsī says that the ground for separation in such cases is the difference of *Dars* or territories and not mere captivity of one of the spouses. Since there is still no difference of the *Dars* in this case as both are still in the same Dar or territory, their original marriage shall continue disregarding the fact whether they were made captive together at the same time or one after another. But if one of the spouses is taken to the Dar al-Islam, separation will take place because of the difference (*tabayun*) of the *Dars*. (See *Mabsut*, vol. X, p. 51).

47. The original term used in the text for 'similar' is *mithli*, which has been translated by some western scholars (e.g., J. Schacht. *Introduction*) as fungible, means a commodity of which the

similar in terms of quality, weight, measure, etc. is easily available in the market for the same price. New motor cars, most of edible items, currency notes of a particular denomination, etc. are to be treated as *mithli* or fungible. As against this, *qimi* or non-fungible is that whose every single unit has its own price and value determined in view of its own quality, size, etc. Cattle, houses of various modes of construction and their locality, land, etc. are to be treated as non-fungible or *qimi* items. It may be pointed out here that *riba*-based transactions are conceivable in loans or exchange of fungible commodities only. (For details see Mustafa Ahmad al-Zarqa, *al-Madkhal li al-Fiqh al-Islami*, 6th edition, vol. III, pp. 130-143).

48. The reference here is to the legal concept known as *al-Qawlu li man* (literally: whose is the saying). The principle is that if both the parties in a litigation are unable to produce evidence, the person whose position is supported by the apparent situation (*zahir al-hal)* will be called upon to make statement on oath which will be accepted. The evidence will be required only from such a party who is claiming something contrary to the apparent. (See, for further details, Ali Haydar, Durar al-Ḥukkām, vol. IV, pp. 492-504).

49. Declaration of the manumission of a slave on the death of the master was technically known as tadbir; a slave so promised freedom was called *mudabbar*. The principle followed in case of tadbir was that a *Mudabbar* slave could neither be sold to anybody nor gifted away. However, the master had every right to utilize the services of a *mudabbar* slave as allowed under the law of the Shari'ah. Further, the principle of *tadbir* was subject to the laws of inheritance and wills that restrict the

will up to one-third of the total property bequeathed. As such, if the value of the *mudabbar* exceeded one-third of the total value of the property bequeathed, the excess was to be paid by the *Mudabbar* after his manumission to the heirs of the deceased master. The law gave much respite to the *mudabbar* to pay this excess amount at his convenience.

50. Dowry or compensation to be paid to a woman in case of sexual intercourse in a voidable or irregular marriage or relationship to a slave- girl is called 'uqr. Under Islamic law sexual intercourse with any woman necessitates one of the three things: mahr or marriage-gift to be paid by the husband to the wife in case of a valid marriage, 'uqr or compensation to be paid to a slave-girl in case of an irregular relationship as explained above or *hadd* punishment.
51. Arsh means a compensation to be paid by the offenders to the victim or his heirs in case of bodily injuries. The Islamic law has specified different amounts of money to be paid as such compensation for different kinds and degrees of hurts/injuries. See, for details, 'Abd al-Qadir 'Awdah, al-Tashri' al-lina'i al-Islami (Beirut, n.d.). vol. II, 261-288.
52. *Al-Jami' al-Kabir* is one of the six most important works of Shaybānī known as *Zahir al-Riwayah* which constitutes the basis of all subsequent development of Hanafi *Fiqh.*
53. The words possession and acquisition have been used to convey the sense of *ihraz* for which see nn. 36 and 41 above.
54. Security is the translation of *aman*, a kind of temporary or permanent security permit issued by the Islamic state to a non- Muslim resident of an alien, mostly belligerent, state. A person holding *aman* is known as *musta'min.* See for details,

'Abd al- Karim Zaydän, Ahkām al- Dhimmiyyin wa'l- Musta'minin and the School of Islam (Beirut- Baghdad, 1982).

55. "Guaranteed Citizen" is the translation of the term Ahl al- *Dhimmah*, the non- Muslim residents of the Islamic State. Since their lives and property have been guaranteed, they are known as the Ahl al- *Dhimmah* or the Dhimmis. See for details, 'Abd al- Karim Zaydan, The Rules of *al- Dhimmiyyin*, op. cit.
56. *Harbi*, literally belligerent, means the citizen of a state at war with the Muslim state, actually or theoretically. The latter case includes a state with which no agreement of peace or armistice, etc. exists. For details see Muhammad Hamidullah, The Muslim Conduct of State op. cit. pp. 111-19.
57. In fact, the principle is that a child found in the Territory of Islam shall be presumed to be Muslim if he has no parents or has at least one Muslim parent with him in the Territory of Islam. But if he is found in the Territory of War with no parents or with non-Muslim parents in the Territory of Islam, he will be considered to be non-Muslim. The rule is that the child follows the religion of his parents. If both have the same religion or in case the parents belong to different religious, he will follow the religion of the parent whose religion is better. In case he has no parents then the religion of the Territory (*Dar*) will be presumed to be the religion of the child. See, for further discussion, Sarakhsī, *al-Mabsut*, vol. X, in loco.
58. *Udul* is the plural of '*adl*. Literally just, equitable and balanced, technically *adl* means a normally upright person whose evidence is acceptable in an Islamic court. Muslim jurists have discussed the concept of '*adl* at length in the context of the law of evidence. For some such discussion see, *'Ali Haydar,*

Durar al-Hukkam, vol. IV, pp. 359-360; *Khalid al-Atāsī, Sharh Majallat al-Ahkam al-'Adliyyah* (Quetta, 1403 AH), vol. V, pp. 282-290.

59. The phrase "... fully protected" is the translation of the term *mumiana* i.e., the one having *mana'ah* which signifies the security available to a belligerent which protects him from being subdued by the Muslim army. Islamic law distinguishes between an enemy individual enjoying *mana'ah* and an enemy individual not enjoying *mana'ah* on many counts.
60. *Kaffarah*, or religious expiation, is a kind of compulsory charity to be performed by an offender in order to seek forgiveness of his sin on the Day of Judgement. Normally, it involves manumission of a slave, preferably a Muslim, or, failing which fasting for a given period or, failing which, to feed a given number of the poor. *Kaffarah* is performed in such offences where either there is no or lesser criminal intention on the part of the offender or where the offence is basically of a moral nature.
61. *Diyah* means blood-money. The Shari'ah has given an elaborate law on the payment of *Diyah*, its amount and rate in various situations, the liability to pay it and the mode of its payment. This law is mostly based on a written memorandum addressed by the Holy Prophet (peace be on him) to his governor in Yemen, Abu Bakr Muhammad ibn 'Amr ibn Hazm. For the text of the Memorandum see Muhammad Hamidullah, *al- Watha'iq al-Siyasiyyah*, in loco.
62. For *Mudabbar* see nn. 49 above.
63. *Umm Walad*, literally 'mother of the child', means a slave-girl who gives birth to the child of her master. According to Islamic law, as soon as a slave-girl gives birth to the child of

her master, she acquires some special privileges. She becomes like a *mudabbar* (see nn. 49 above) to be automatically manumitted on the death of the master. An *ummu walad* can neither be sold to anybody nor her ownership can be transferred to anybody. But unlike a *muddabbar*, an *ummu walad* shall not be liable to pay any excess amount to the heirs of the master if her price/value exceeds one-third of the total inheritance of the master. For details see *al-Marghinani, Hidayah*, vol. 4, Book on *Istilad.*

64. The author here tries to differentiate between two situations: a peaceful legal entry by a Muslim soldier in the *Dar al-Harb* with permission of security and his entry in the *Dar al-Harb* as part of hostile and belligerent activities. In the first case, he has to abide by the provisions of the contract or agreement with the *Dar al-Harb* and to respect the sanctity of their life and property so much so that his own property taken possession by the *Harbis* will be treated by him to be their legitimate property. In the second case, however, he has full justification to harm the enemy in any possible way. For details see Sarakhsï, *al-Mabsut*, vol. X, pp. 65-66.

65. *Fay'* is the enemy property coming to the Muslims without any warlike operation. Based on the verses 59: 6-7, the commentators of the Qur'an and the jurists have developed elaborate law on the question of *fay'*. See, for details, inter alia, *al-Qurtubi, al-Jami' li Ahkam al-Qur'an*, II edition (Cairo, n.d.), vol. XVIII, pp. 10-33; al-Mawardī, *al-Ahkam al-Sultaniyyah* (Cairo, 1966), pp. 136-152. Abu Yusuf, *Kitab al-Kharāj* (Cairo, n.d.), pp. 25-45. See also Abu 'Ubayd. *Kitab al-Amwal*. Yahya ibn Adam, *Kitab al-Kharaj* (Lahore, 1395 AH), pp. 15-56.

66. Muslim jurists attached much importance to the Dar (literally, a house, residence or territory, but technically something closer to nationality in this context). In many cases the matter is decided on the basis of the Dar of the person concerned at the time of his conversion to Islam or the conquest of a territory. For detailed arguments in support of the views given in the text see, Sarakhsī, *Mabsut*, vol. X, pp. 66-69.
67. For technical meaning of the term acquisition or *ihraz* see notes 34, 36, 41.
68. This ruling is based on a report according to which the Holy Prophet (peace be on him) has said: "Whoever enters the fold of Islam [and accepts the citizenship of the Islamic state] along with some property, it will be [recognized to be] his property". This hadith, in fact, gives a basic principle of the private International Law of Islam which recognizes all contracts, ownerships and other legal instruments recognized by other legal systems in respect of their citizens. It is because of this principle that the marriage, divorce, parentage, ownership, etc. of a person in a non-Muslim country according to the law of that country are accepted as valid at the time of his conversion to Islam or his acceptance of the citizenship of the Islamic State.
69. This manumission in the Territory of War will be considered to be null and void for the purposes of *wala'* i.e., clientship or allegiance, a kind of special association between the manumitter and the manumitted which continued throughout their life and, in some respects, was virtually a kind of blood-relationship entitling even to inherit in some cases. For details about *wala'* see following sources:

i) Sarakhsi, al- Mabsu, vol. VIII, pp. 81--125.

ii) Kāsāni, Bada'i' al- Sana'i', vol. IV, pp. 159-173.

iii) Kamal ibn Humam, Fath al- Qadir, vol. VIII (Quetta, n.d.), pp. 152-165.

iv) Ibn Qudamah, al- Mughni (Riyadh, Imam Muhammad ibn Sa'ūd University), vol. VI, pp. 348-381.

v) Sharbīnī, Mughni al- Muhtāj, (*Dar al- Fikr*, n.d.) Vol. IV,pp 506-508.

70. *Istibra'* literally means to secure absolution or freedom from liability; but technically, in the context of the law of slavery, it means a waiting period to ascertain whether or not a slave-girl is pregnant and in case of pregnancy, *istibra'* would mean waiting till the birth of the child and the passage of the post-natal period of confinement.

71. The author is here discussing a case where, during a war, a group of Muslim soldiers enters the enemy territory without the specific permission of the commander and gets some booty. Shaybānī says that since the force or strength which had given them the courage to enter the enemy territory comes from the entire army which is the *sine qua non* of their success, therefore, the whole army will have a right in the booty.

72. *Maṣisah or Missisah* is a town in Syria. *Malatiyah or Malatiyyah* is a town in the West of Euphrates.

73. Scriptuary is an English rendering of the Arabic term *Kitabi* which means a person belonging to *Ahl al-Kitab* or People of the Book which is the Qur'anic term for Jews, Christians and Sabians.

74. For the meaning of *Istibra'* see nn. 70 above.

75. The Qur'an (4:101) allows the believers to reduce to a half the length of the three longest ones of the daily prayers while in a journey. The purpose is to provide a concession to the travelers by reducing the number of *rak'ahs* from four to two as long as one is on a journey. Muslim jurists have made elaborate discussions on the conditions of this reduction in terms of the distance and duration of the journey, etc. For further details see Wahbah al-Zuhayli, *al-Fiqh al-Islami wa Adillatuhu* (Damascus, 1984), vol. II, pp. 315-360.
76. Many jurists are of the view that the prescribed punishments (hudud) should not be imposed in the territory of the enemy lest the offender deserts to the enemy. But Shaybānī is of the view that if the Muslim army is to punish the offender without incurring the risk of his desertion, the *Hadd* punishment can be imposed in the territory of the enemy. This will, however, be at the discretion of the commander.
77. *Kharaj* was a levy on the agricultural produce taken mostly from the non- Muslim citizens and was parallel to *'ushr* or tithe taken from Muslims. The amount of *Kharaj* was much less than that of *'Ushr.* For details, *Diya' al-Din al-Rayyis, al-Kharaj fi'l-Dawlah al-Islamiyyah,* op. cit.
78. *Qafiz or qafiz,* a measure of capacity equal to forty liters of wheat (approximately) according to the calculation of the Hanafis and thirty- three liters according to others.
79. Jarib, a measure of land as well as of edible commodities. In the case of land, it is equal to 1366.0416 square metres, and in the case of food, it is equal to 132 litres (circa).
80. "Old" is the translation of the term shaykh fani; literally the 'dying old' or 'expiring old'. it Technically it means an old person who is physically unable to perform his religious

obligations, such as prayer or fasting, and is not expected to ever regain strength to perform them later.

81. "Disabled" is the translation of the term muq'ad, literally stopped or brought to a standstill or made seated; crippled or invalid.
82. See n. 43 above.
83. *Makruh* or disliked is an act omission or commission neither ordered nor forbidden by the Shariah but merely discouraged or disliked. If a person commits it, he will not be accountable on the Day of Judgement but if he abstains from it, he will receive a reward for his abstention.
84. *Taghlibite*, a person belonging to the tribe of Banu Taghlib, an Arab Christian tribe which had settled down in the area between Iraq and Syria long before Islam and whose leaders were recognized as tributary rulers of an Arab state under the suzerainty of the eastern Roman empire. On the conquest of their area by 'Umar, they had refused to pay the *jizyah* but expressed their willingness to pay double the amount of *zakah* was accepted by 'Umar, setting down a precedent for his successors to enter into such arrangements with other categories of non-Muslims. There are distinct provisions in early books on Islamic law about the *Taghlibites*. This precedent shows that *jizyah* may be dropped in favor of any other financial contribution agreed upon between the Islamic state and a non-Muslim community.
85. See nn. 40 and 77 above.
86. *'Ushr* is the *Zakah* payable on agricultural produce of a Muslim at the rate one tenth or one twentieth in various cases.
87. See n. 43 above.

88. Haram, literally a sanctuary, means a specific area around the Ka'bah, the Cubic House of Allah in Makkah. The boundaries of the Haram were identified by the Holy Prophet (peace be on him) himself but the act of sanctification itself is attributed to the Prophet Ibrāhīm. It existed before the migration of the Holy Prophet to Madinah and its mention is found in the Makkan surahs (See, for example, Qur'an 29:57; 28:57).
89. Peace or *sulh* is used as a term of Fiqh for a permanent peace treaty with the non-Muslims who accept the military and political suzerainty of the Islamic state. The area inhabited by such non-Muslims is called *Dar al- Sulh* or the Territory of Peace.
90. Armistice or *muwada'ah* is a kind of temporary ceasefire for a definite period which should not, according to the Hanafi jurists, be more than ten years in one single instance.
91. This ruling is based on the principle that the Islamic State shall recognize its non-Muslim citizens as the lawful owners of whatever they possessed and claimed to own at the time of acquisition of such citizenship and as such, when these non-Muslims embrace Islam, their titles to their properties shall continue to be recognized. According to Sarakhsi (*al-mabsut*, vol. X, p. 85) his entry into Islam should only strengthen his title rather than weaken it. See also note n. 68 above.
92. *Qisas*, literally to cut off, to trim, to follow, to avenge, and to retaliate; in the terminology of Islamic law, it means punishment by causing a similar hurt at the same part of the body of the offender as he had caused to the victim, or by causing his death if he has committed murder, in exercise of the right of the victim or his heir(s). See, for details *'Abd al-*

Qadir Awdah, al-Tashri al-Jina'i al-Islami, op. cit. vol. II, pp. 113-204, 213-259.

93. *Diyah* is blood-money paid by the offender to the heirs of the victim in cases of murder. For details see *'Abd al- Qadir Awdah, al- Tashri'*, op. city pp. 189-199, 201, 261-288.
94. *Qasamah* is a kind of collective oath taken by the selected representatives of a locality where a blind murder takes place. For details see *'Abd al- Qadir Awdah, al-Tashri'*, pp. 321-341.
95. *Musta'min* literally means a seeker of security, but technically it means a citizen of a (non-Muslim) foreign state entering the Islamic state temporarily with permission to stay up to one year. For fuller details see 'Abd al- Karim Zaydan, *Ahkam al-Dhimmiyyin wa'l- Musta'minin fi Dar al- Islam* (Baghdad, 1982), pp. 46-56; 70-75; 111-136; and passim. See also Muhammad Hamidullah, Muslim Conduct of State, p. 202-204 (paragraphs 415-420).
96. *Tadbir*, a mode of manumission of slaves; see nn. 49 above.
97. See nn. 54 and 95 above.
98. For a short definition of juristic preference or *Istihsan*, see note 45.
99. The question whether or not the evidence of a non-Muslim against a Muslim is admissible in an Islamic court has been the subject of much discussion throughout the fourteen hundred years. Basing their arguments on the literal interpretation of some *ahadith*, the majority of the jurists are of the view that in normal conditions it is inadmissible. For a dissenting view see Ibn Qayyim, *al-Turuq al-Hukmiyyah fil-Siyasah al- Shar'iyyah* (Beirut, n.d.), pp. 157-173.
100. Beast of burden is the translation of the word kura' which literally means foot of an animal whose meat is eaten,

specially sheeps and goats. As an extended meaning the word is also used for horses, mules and donkeys.

101. For some early references relevant to the Islamic concept of contraband see Muhammad Hamidullah, The Muslim Conduct of State, pp. 195-198. For further juristic discussion of the concept see Sarakhsī, *al-mabsut*, vol. X, pp. 91-92, 88-89; idem, Sharh al- Siyar al- Kabir (Cairo, 1971), Vol. 3, pp. 1049-1050; Vol. IV, pp. 1242, 1243, 1410; Vol. V. pp. 1873-1874; 'Ala' al- *Din* al- Kasānī, Bada'i al- Ṣana'i', vol. VII, p. 102; Ibn Qudāmah, al-Mughni, vol. VIII. p. 407.
102. This ruling is based on two principles, viz. that the life and property of a Musta'min is protected in the territory of the Islamic State and that a person embracing Islam and desiring to settle down in the Islamic state shall not be forced to leave the Islamic State. In this ruling Shaybānī tries to fulfil the requirements of both the obligations.
103. See n. 19 above.
104. This ruling is based on the principle that during the period of hostile relations and belligerency the enemy property has no sanctity and any soldier of the Muslim army who captures it shall be entitled thereto under the principle of salab See nn. 44 above.
105. For a brief definition of Haram see nn. 88 above.
106. Hill (literally permission) is the area between the *Miqat* (or specified points around the city of Makkah beyond which an outsider cannot go with the ceremonial dress of *Ihram*) and the Haram area. For a detailed discussion on Haram and Hill lands see Sayyid Zawwar Husayn, *'Umdat al-Fiqh* (Karachi, 1979), vol. IV, pp. 81-113.

107. This ruling is based on the concept of *ihraz.* (See nn. 34, 41 above), which allows the acquisition of enemy's property during the war provided no treachery is involved. The concept behind this principle is that the successful acquisition of a lawful property is a valid source of ownership; for example, a hunter who hunts an animal not owned by somebody and whose hunting is lawful becomes lawful owner of the hunted animal as soon as he successfully acquires it. On the basis of the same principle, Abū Ḥanifah allows the receipt (not payment) of usurious increase and profits by a Muslim in a transaction with a *Harbi* concluded in the *Dar al-Harb.*

108. Hanafi jurists allow some transactions in *Dar al-Harb* but not in Dar al- Islam because such transactions have a territorial (as against personal) application. *Qisas* and other criminal laws are, basically, applicable to a citizen of the Islamic state and not to a foreign visitor. Moreover, since a *Harbi* being a belligerent has, initially, no guarantee as to his life and property, he cannot enjoy the same protection of law as does a permanent non-Muslim citizen.

109. See n. 93 above.

110. Under Islamic law, a male slave cannot have more than two wives at the same time. In the situation contemplated in the text, a person marries four women at the same time and it is difficult to identify as to who are the first two whom he married, all his marriages must be considered null and void as soon as he becomes a slave, because as a slave he can retain only two. However, if he marries them at different times, the first two shall remain his wives while the marriages with the two wives whom he married later shall be treated as

terminated forthwith. See, for further discussion, Sarakhsī, *al-Mabsut*, vol. X, pp. 96-97.

111. For a detailed discussion on the question of slaughter see Wahbah al- Zuḥayli, al-Fiqh al-Islāmi wa Adillatuhu, vol. III, pp. 647-688.

112. This ruling is based on the principle of reciprocity on which many rules of the international law of Islam are to be based. Since the *Harbi*s who kill a Muslim are not liable to pay any compensation, likewise, a Muslim should not be liable to pay any compensation if he kills a *Harbi* in the Territory of War. For some discussion on the principle of Reciprocity see Muhammad Hamidullah, Muslim Conduct of State, pp. 33, 135, who also mentions some earlier sources.

113. This ruling is based on the differentiation made by Muslim jurists between an action of a Muslim involving a treachery with the *Harbi* and an action not involving treachery. In the first case, since there was a possibility of a doubt whether or not the act was based on treachery, Shaybānī does not allow concubinage but in the latter case, there being no such doubt, Shaybānī allows such purchase and subsequent concubinage.

114. This ruling is again based on a common consideration of the principles of *ihraz* and the prohibition of treachery.

115. *Muwada'ah* (armistice or friendship) has been used here for the friendly relationship between the Muslim state and a non-Muslim state based on mutual respect and friendship. Sometime the term is used for a temporary armistice between two belligerent states. See also n. 90 above.

116. The whole concept underlying this ruling may appear to some people to be curious as it is basically opposed to the western concept of territorial nationalism. But Islamic law

and polity is based on the belief in the ideology of Islam according to which it is only the defense of one's life, honor, property or (religious) ideology for which a war is justified. A Muslim is allowed to take arms only in self-defense or where a war is fought for the purpose of serving Allah's cause where the law of Islam is supreme.

117. Islamic law is very sensitive about honoring the covenant pledged to the non-Muslim citizens of the Islamic state. There are several sayings of the Holy Prophet which require the Muslims to honor the pledge given to the non-Muslims. For some such sayings of the Holy Prophet see Amin Abḥsan Iṣlāhī, Islami Riyasat (Lahore, 1977), pp. 197-99; see also pp. 204-209; 209-213; 222-23. See also Ab'l-A'la Mawdūdī, Islāmi Riyasat (Lahore, 1988), pp. 577-78, 580-81.

118. The difference with the Khawarij notwithstanding, the unity and solidarity of the ummah requires that any foreign (non-Muslim) aggression against any Muslim group should be taken as an aggression against the whole body of the Muslims.

119. There is a unanimity among the jurists of all schools that an apostate should be given an opportunity to get his doubts and misgivings about Islam clarified. Since the ground norm in Islamic law is the total submission and surrender before the revealed guidance brought by the Holy Prophet Muhammad (peace be on him), the Shari'ah of the Prophet represents good par excellence, Truth par excellence, and Justice par excellence and ensures the ultimate happiness both in this world and in the Hereafter. Islam does not accept the contention that anybody can have any insoluble question about the fundamental teachings of Islam that would lead him to apostasy. For an elaborate discussion see *Ṣāliḥ al-*

Smarra'i, Ahkam al-Murtad, Beirut any compendium on Islamic Fiqh, in loco.

In recent decades some modernist writers in the Muslim world have questioned the legitimacy of capital punishment for apostasy simplicitaire. For a representative elaboration of this view see S.A. Rahman, The Punishment of Apostasy in Islam. (Lahore, 1973). The Qadianis have also, for obvious reasons, been in the forefront of those who doubted the justification of capital punishment for apostasy simplicitaire. Their scholars, Zafarullah, Muhammad Ali and others, have produced bulky literature on this issue.

120. The presumption about an apostate is that either he re-embraces Islam or faces execution or flees away from the Muslim land. In the last case, he is presumed to be dead the moment he enters the Territory of War. For details see Muhammad Hamidullah, Muslim Conduct of State, pp. 174-77. See also *Sālih al-Samarra'i, Ahkam al-Murtad.*

121. This is the Hanafi point of view which presumes him to be dead the moment he apostatizes. But according to al-Shafi'ī, his property shall be treated as *Fay'* (see nn. 65 above) and shall be transferred to the Public Exchequer. Shafi'ī has based his ruling on the well-known hadith which prohibits inheritance between a Muslim and a non-Muslim. See, for detailed discussion) Sarakhsī, al-Mabsut, vol. X, pp. 100-102.

122. The manumission of such slave-girls on the actual or constructive death of the master is an established principle of Islamic law based on several traditions attributed to the Holy Prophet and the Second Caliph, 'Umar. See, for details, *Ibn Humām, Fath al-Qadir*, chapter on *Istilad*; see also other standard compendia on Fiqh, chapters on *Istilad, Umm Walad or Ummahat al-Awlad.*

123. See nn. 11 and 49 above.

124. See n. 49 above.

125. See n. 43 above.

126. This ruling is based on the principle that the establishment of parentage constitutes one of the primary objectives of the Shariah and should have precedence over any other consideration. See, for details, Sarakhsī, al- Mabsūt, vol. X, pp. 104-106.

127. Islamic law had recognized the manumitter as an heir in the absence of other cognate (*'asabah*) heirs. See chapters on Wala' or *Muwalah* in and standard Fiqh compendium. See also n. 69 above.

128. See n. 65 above.

129. Actions taken by a sick man (on his death-bed) in respect of the disposal of his property shall be subject to the outcome of his illness: if he dies during that illness, his actions shall be valid only subject to the law of wills and inheritance, e.g., up to a maximum of one-third, etc.; if he recovers, then all his actions are valid and shall have effect accordingly.

130. In cases of unintentional homicide, the Islamic law requires that the *Diyah* shall be payable by the *'aqilah* of the offender. During the early days of Islam, the male adult cognate (*'asabah*) relatives of an offender were required to share the burden of the payment of money. Later on, Caliph 'Umar ruled that with the change in the social structure, it should not only be the *'asabah* who should constitute the *'aqilah* of a person but also all those who are normally expected to provide him any help in moments of need should be included

in the definition of *'aqilah.* This ruling is the basis of the Hanafi concept of *'aqilah* which defines it in broader terms. According to the definition proposed by the Council of Islamic Ideology of Pakistan, a constitutional body to advise the Parliament on matters of Islamic law, the *'aqilah* of a person are those "male, adult, and sane members of his tribe, group or class of persons, association, organization, institution, company, corporation, establishment, department, trade union or family through which that person receives or expects to receive help and support in moments of crisis or hour of need". For details about *'aqilah* see chapters on *ma'aqil 'awaqil or 'aqilah* in the compendia of Figs. For a discussion on the rationale of the principle of 'äqilah see the present writer's article "*Qisas wa Diyat ke Chand Pehlu*" in *Fikr wa Nazar,* Islamabad (April 1984). See also the present writer, (ed.) *Musawwadah Qanun- i- Qisas wa Diyat* (Islamabad, 1984).

131. For reasons of this ruling see Sarakhsi, *al-Mabsut*, vol. X. p. 107.
132. In the text the term ghasb has been used which means to take a valid property into unauthorized possession without the permission of the owner by depriving the previous possessor of his valid possession; see chapter on Ghash in any standard book of *Fiqh.*
133. "Unprotected by law" is the translation of the term hadr or hadar which means going unretaliated and uncompensated of a murder or hurt. 134. Arsh is used for a part of the *diyat* payable in cases of hurts.
134. In some cases, the word *diyat* is used in place of arsh but not vice versa.

135. *'Iddah* is the waiting period during which a divorced woman or a widow cannot remarry. The purpose is to ensure that the divorcee or the widow is not pregnant in which case she will have to wait till the birth of the child. This is prescribed in order to avoid any possible confusion concerning the parentage of the child about which the Shari'ah is very sensitive.

136. This ruling is based on the principle (entertained by the Hanafi jurists) that the difference of the Dar or territory is a valid ground for a separation between the spouses. For details see Sarakhsi, *al-Mabsut*, vol. X, pp. 115-117.

137. Shaykh fani is that old person who has become virtually invalid because of old age and there is no probability of his regaining strength.

138. See n. 39 above.

139. See n. 43 above.

140. This ruling is based on the principle that the homicide of a person already liable to be killed is not considered to be a murder or culpable homicide and, hence, the offender is not liable to *qisas* or *diyat*. He may, however, be prosecuted for taking the law in his own hands and may be awarded some punishment therefor by way of ta'zir, provided he proves before a court that the victim was, in fact, liable to execution in terms of Islamic law.

141. See n. 49 above.

142. See n. 63 above.

143. See nn. 92, 108 above.

144. See n. 136 above.

145. *Ismah* literally means protection but in the context of marriage it means the marriage bond which provides a moral,

physical and social protection to spouses particularly to the wife.

146. The term "*Territory of Disbelief*" or "*Dar al-Kufr*" has been used by the jurists in a general sense and includes all territories outside the frontiers of Dar al-Islam. This term shows that Muslim jurists do contemplate a Dar dominated by non-Muslims which may not be considered as *Dar al- Harb* or *Territory of War.*

147. Islamic law provided special injunctions for the idolaters and polytheists of the Arabian Peninsula. Based on the guidance contained in Surah Tawbah the generally accepted position is that the idolaters of Arabia had no option of permanently settling down in Arabia; they had either to accept Islam, or to leave Arabia or to face execution. For details, see Sarakhsi, al-Mabsut, vol. XI, pp. 117-19. For a modern exposition of this principle see *Amin Ahsan Iṣlahi, Tadabbur-i Qur'an*, commentary of *Surah Tawbah*. For a succinct exposition of this view see also his Islāmi Riyāsat, pp. 186-91.

148. *Ahl al-Kitab* or the People of the Book or the Scriptuaries is a term given by the Qur'an to the Christians and the Jews. Islamic law contains special provisions to regulate the relationship between them and the Muslims. In several respects their status in an Islamic State is somewhat in-between the Muslims and other non-Muslims. Later on, pursuant to the guidance contained in some *Ahadith*, some Muslim jurists extended the treatment given to the Jews and the Christians, to the Magians and the Sabians. See, for details, *'Abd al-Karim Zaydan, Aḥkām al-Dhimiyyin*, pp. 11-16.

149. Analogical Reasoning or Qiyas has been the most popular and prevalent mode of Ijtihad and is, as such, considered to

be the fourth source of Islamic law. For a modern elaboration of the principle see Ahmad Hasan, Analogical Reasoning in *Islamic Jurisprudence*, op. cit.

150. This opinion of Abu Yusuf is based on the principle that the actions, disposals and utterances of a child shall be interpreted in a way not prejudicial to his interests. See, Sarakhsī, -al *Mabsut*, vol. X, pp. 122 -23.
151. See n. 45 above.
152. The Hanafi law treats an apostate and a Dhimmi breaking the covenant in the same manner; as soon as they flee from the Territory of Islam, they are presumed to be dead for purposes of the disposal of their property.
153. The Day of the Camel is the day when the well-known battle was fought between the followers of 'Ali and the advocates of retaliation for the murder of 'Uthman, the third Caliph. The battle was led by 'A'ishah, the wife of the Holy Prophet, who was riding a camel, hence the Battle of the Camel or the Day of the Camel.
154. The *People of justice* are those who support the legitimate Islamic government against the rebels.
155. *The People of Rebellion or Ahl al-Baghy* is a term used for those rebels who defy the legimate authority of the Islamic government and establish their own unconstitutional and illegitimate authority.
156. The people of Nahrawan were a group of the Khawarij against whom Ali, the fourth Caliph, had to fight a battle at a place in Iraq known as Nahrawan.
157. For an elaborate discussion on the position of Islamic law about the admissibility of the records and precedents of other courts including those established by the rebels or any

illegitimate authority. See *al- Fatawa al- Hindiyyah* (Beirut, 1986), vol. III, pp. 107-1 381-96; Sarakhsī, *al-mabsut*, pp. 107-1 130-31

158. Prescribed punishments or the *Hudud* are those, five or seventeen, according to different views punishments which have been prescribed in the Quran or the Sunnah for various offences. These include punishments for theft, dacoity, fornication, adultery, apostasy, use of liquor and accusation of illicit sexual intercourse.

159. Islamic law has prescribed special rituals for the funeral of the martyrs i.e., those who lay down their lives in the battlefield in a war fought for the cause of Islam. For details see chapters on Shahid in the part dealing with funeral prayers in any standard Fiqh compendium.

160. "Just" is a term used in the context of a rebellion for those who support the legitimate and the constitutional authority. A just soldier is, therefore, a soldier serving in the army of the legitimate authority and a just qadi is the one appointed by or exercising authority on behalf of the legitimate authority.

161. Because even though the agreement has been made by the rebels who have defied the lawful authority of the legitimate Islamic government, yet the '*People of justice*' are required to honor it because any act contrary to it will amount to a treachery on the part of a group of the Muslims.

162. Khawarij were those supporters of 'Ali who had later deserted him on the plea that he had committed disbelief by accepting an arbitrator in his dispute with Mu'awiyah, for, they maintained, the real arbitrator is only Allah. In the classical Fiqh books, however, the term Khawarij is also used for rebels.

163. Law of justice or *Hukm al-'Adl* means the laws or the instructions issued by a just and legitimate (as against a rebel and illegitimate) authority.

164. For the law of highway man ship, or qatal- tariq, see any standard Fiqh compendium.

165. See n. 130 above.

166. See n. 93 above.

167. See n. 92 above.

168. The principle of one-fifth of the booty going to the public exchequer is based on the Quranic injunction 8:41.

169. These are various terms used for the religious devout of mostly Christian religion. "Monk" is the translation of *Rahib or Mutarahhib*; "residents of hermitages" is the translation of Ashab al-Sawami' while "cross strip-wearers" is the translation of *Ashab al-Zunnar*.

170. This ruling is based on the consideration that in matters of Halal and Haram, Islamic Law has a personal rather than territorial application. The principle in this behalf is that a Muslim is bound by the laws of Islam wherever he may be. (Cf. Sarakhsī, al-Mabsut, vol. X, p. 95).

171. This question shows that according to Muslim jurists all non-Muslims were not included in the *People of war* (as some modern writers try to make their readers believe).

172. Arsh is a term used for the *diyat* of the organs or the limbs. It is always determined with reference to the full *diyat*: half, one-fourth etc.

173. See n. 49 above.

174. See n. 43 above.

175. See n. 63 above.

176. All these rulings are based on two principles. (1) Actions and transactions made by the non-Muslims before accepting Islam or the Guarantee shall be accepted as valid by the Islamic government. (2) Anybody who accepts Islam or the *Guarantee* along with a property claimed by him to be his property shall be recognized to be the owner of that property.

Bibliography

Abdur Rahim. *The Principles of Muhammadan Jurisprudence*. Lahore, n.d.

Abu 'Ubayd, al- Qasim ibn Sallam. *Kitab al- Amwal*. Islamabad, 1986.

Abu Yusuf, *al- Radd 'ala Siyar al- Awza't*. Ed. *Abu'l Wafa' al- Afghānī*. Cairo, n.d.

Aghnides, Nocolas P. An Introduction to Muhammedan Theories of Finance. Lahore, 1981.

Ansari, Zafar Ishaq. "An Early Discussion on Islamic Jurisprudence". Some Notes on *al-Radd 'ala Siyar al-Awza't,* in Khurshid Ahmad and Zafar Ishaq Ansari, (eds.), Islamic Perspectives. Leicester and Jeddah, 1979.

Arsalan, Shakib. Ed. *Mahasin al- Masa'i fi Manaqib al- Imam al- Awzat*. Cairo, n.d.

Al- Atasi, Khalid. *Sharh Majallat al- Ahkam al-'Adliyyah,* Vol. V. Quetta, 1403 AH.

Austin, John. *Lectures on Jurisprudence*. Vol. I. London, 1873.

'Awdah, *'Abd al- Qadir, Al- Tashri' al- Jina'i al- Islami,* Beirut, n.d.

Al- Baghdadi, *Al- Khatib*. Ta'rikh Baghdad. Vol. II. Cairo, 1931.

Al- Baladhuri, Ahmad ibn 'Isa ibn Jabir, *Futuḥ al- Buldan*. Leiden, 1866.

Al- Bukhari, Muhammad Ibn Ibrahim. *Al- Jami' al- Sahih* (*Kitab al- Hiyal*).

Al- Dhahabi, Shams al- *Din* Muhammad ibn Ahmad. *Mizan al- I'tidal.* Vol. III. Shaikhupura, 1963.

Al- Fazarı, Ibrahim. *Kitab al- Siyar.* Ed. Faruq Hammudah, Beirut, 1987. Ghazi, Mahmood Ahmad. "*Qisaş wa Diyat kay Chand Pahlu, Fikr wa Nazar.* April, 1984.

Musawwadh-'i Qanun- i Qisas wa Diyat. Islamabad, 1984. *Al- Hamawi, Yaqut. Mu'jam al- Buldan.* Vol. V. Beirut, 1984.

Hamidullah, Muhammad. *Ahd-i Nabawi mén Nizam-i-Hukmrāni.* Karachi, 1981.

The Muslim Conduct of State. Lahore, 1973.

Al-Watha'iq al-Siyasiyyah. Beirut.

Hasan, Ahmad. Analogical Reasoning in *Islamic Jurisprudence.* Islamabad, 1986.

Haydar, Ali. *Durar al- Hukkām.* Baghdad, n.d.

Husayn, Sayyid Zawwar. *'Umdat al- Fiqh.* Karachi, 1979.

Ibn Abidin. Rasa 'il Ibn 'Abidin. Lahore, 1963.

Ibn Hajar, Ahmad ibn 'Ali ibn Hajar. *Fatih al- Bari.* Vol. XII. Beirut, 1985.

Tahdhib al- Tahdhib. Vol. IX. Hyderabad, 1326-27.

Ibn Humām, Kamal. *Fatih al- Qadir.* Vol. VII. Quetta, n.d.

Ibn Khallikan, Shams al- *Din* Abu '1 'Abbas Ahmad ibn Ibrahim. *Wafayat al- A'yan.* Vol. I. Cairo, 1368 AH.

Ibn Nujaym. *Al-Bahr al Ra'iq.* Beirut, n.d., reprinted in Quetta, n.d.

Ibn Qayyim al- Jawziyyah, Muḥammad ibn Abi Bakr. *Ahkam Ahl al- Dhimmah*. Ed. Subhi Ṣāliḥ, Beirut, 1981.

Al- Turuq al- Hukmiyyah fi'l Siyasah al- Shar'iyyah. Beirut, n.d.

Ibn Qudamah, Muwaffaq al- *Din* Abu Muhammad Abd Allah ibn Ahmad. Al- Mughni. Vol. VI. Riyadh, n.d.

Islahi, Amin Ahsan. *Islamic Riyasat*. Lahore, 1977.

Tadabbur- i Qur'an. Lahore, 1983. *Al- Fatawa al- Hindiyyah*. Beirut, 1986.

Al- Jassas, al- Razi Abu Bakr Ahmad ibn 'Ali. *Ahkam al- Quran*, Vol. I. Cairo, 1347 AH.

Kapoor, S.K., and Tandon, L.N. *International Law*. Lahore, 1980.

Al- Kāsānī, Abu Bakr Mas'ud. *Bada'i al-'Sana'i'*. Karachi, 1400 AH.

Al- Kawthari, Muhammad Zahid. *Bulugh al- Amani fi Sirat al- Imam Muhammad ibn al- Hasan al- Shaybānī*. Hims, 1969.

Khadduri, Majid. The Islamic Law of Nations: Shaybānī's Sale. Baltimore, 1966.

Kruse, Hans, "*The Foundations of Islamic International Jurisprudence*", Journal of Pakistan History Society. October, 1955.

"*Al-Shaybānī on International Instruments*". Journal of Pakistan History Society. Vol. I, 1953.

Lakhnawi, *Abd al- Hayy. Al- Ta'liq al- Mumajjad*. Lucknow, 1925.

Mawdūdi, Abu'l A'lā. *Islamic Riyāsat*. Lahore, 1988.

Al- Mawardi, Abu'l- Hasan Ali ibn Muhammad. *Al- Ahkam al- Sultaniyyah*, Cairo, 1966.

Oppenhein, J. *International Law*. London, 1955.

Paton, G.W. A Textbook of *Jurisprudence*. Oxford, 1954.

Al- Qurtubi Abu Abd Allah Muhammad ibn Ahmad. *Al- Jami' li Ahkām al- Qur'an*. Cairo, n.d.

Rahman, S.A. The Punishment of Apostasy in Islam. Lahore, 1973.

Al- Rayyis, *Diya' al- Din. Al- Kharaj fi'l- Dawlah al- Islamiyyah.* Cairo, 1951. Salmond. Jurisprudence. London, 1966.

Al- Samarra, Salih. *Ahkam al- Murtadd*. Beirut, n.d.

Al- Sarakhsi, Abu Bakr Muhammad ibn Abi Sahl Ahmad. *Al- Mabsut* Kabul, 1405 AH.

Saymari Abi Hanifah newspaper. Lahore, 1968.

Sezgin, Fuat. History of Arabic literature. Vol. I. Leiden, 1967.

Shafi, Muhammad ibn Idris. *Kitab al- Umm*. Beirut, 1973.

Al- S*Harbi*ni, Muhammad Khatib. Mughni'l- Muhtaj. Damascus, *Dar al- Fikr,* n.d.

Al- Shaybānī, Muḥammad ibn al- Hasan. *Al- Makhārij fi'l- Hiyal*, Schacht, Jospeph, ed. Baghdad, n.d.

Starke, J.G. An Introduction to International Law. London, 1972.

Al- Ṭabarī, Ibn Jarir. *Ikhtilaf al- Fuqaha'*. Ed. J. Schacht. Berlin, 1933.

Tu*fay*l, Muhammad. Nuqush, Seerat Number, Vol. XI. Lahore, 1985.

Yahya ibn Adam. *Kitab al- Kharaj*. Lahore, 1395 AH.

Yusufuddin, Muhammad. Islam is not safe. Karachi, 1984.

Al-Zarqa, Mustafa Ahmad. *Al- Madkhallila al- Fiqh al- Islami.* 6th ed. Damascus,1968.

Zaydan, 'Abd al- Karim. *Ahkam al- Dhimmiyyin wa'l- Musta'minin in Dar al- Islam.* Beirut- Baghdad, 1982.

Al- Zubayli, Wahbah. *Al- Fiqh al- Islami wa Adillatuhu.* Damascus, 1984.

www.ingramcontent.com/pod-product-compliance
Lightning Source LLC
Chambersburg PA
CBHW050527240926
51846CB00003B/723
* 9 7 8 8 1 1 9 9 4 6 1 6 7 *